God's Will
still Is
Prosperity!

Dr. Stan Wangenye

PRESS

DEDICATION

———⟨∞⟩———

I dedicate this book to the following *very* special people:

To my darling wife, Jemi Wangenye,
Co Pastor, Eagles' Gathering Christian Centre, London, An exceptional woman of excellence, diligence and integrity. A delightful jewel and gift from God to me, our children and to all those who know and love her. *Jemi, all this would not have been possible without you!*

AND

To Pastors Wade & Carla Porter,
Living Faith International, Nairobi, Kenya.
You've natured my wife and I as our Spiritual parents over the years and your tremendous input into our lives brings Glory to our Heavenly Father. My wife and I are humbled by your great love and we honor you.

AND

To Dr. Jerry J. Savelle,
Jerry Savelle Ministries International, Crowley, TX.
I'm eternally grateful for the heritage and spirit of faith that both my wife and I have received from your mentorship. I honor you for the gift of God you are to us and to the body of Christ.

TABLE OF CONTENTS

SECTION 3
Keys to receive from God 147

SECTION 4
The Purpose of Godly wealth 169

ENDORSEMENT

———∞∞∞———

When anyone accepts Jesus Christ as their Lord and Savior, that person experiences the tremendous miracle of being born again into the kingdom of God, with all its rights, privileges, and blessings contained within the inheritance of our prosperity. It is God's desire for us to know Him intimately and to allow the Holy Spirit to reveal the wisdom and knowledge we need to live our lives in the blessings of His prosperity.

There has been much confusion in the body of Christ about whether or not God truly desires to bless and prosper His people. Dr. Stan Wangenye addresses these issues by taking the reader directly to God's Word, leading us through scripture after scripture, and revealing the magnitude of the Lord's plans and purposes for us.

Please read *God's Will Is Still Prosperity* with an open heart and mind. It holds the promise of a great future for you and your family – one that only God can grant you.

Pastor Wade Porter
Senior Pastor,
Victory Faith Church, Nairobi, Kenya

ENDORSEMENT

———∞———

The subject of PROSPERITY is one that has been treated with suspicion in many quarters. In the church, when the word 'prosperity' is mentioned from the pulpit, believers become uncomfortable, mainly due to the fact that prosperity has erroneously been linked to Christians giving all their money to the preacher! This attitude is as a result of erroneous and manipulative teaching on the subject. As a result, this has brought a resistance in the minds of the believers from receiving authentic information. Many in the church have missed the very essence of God's desire and ability to prosper them!

In God's will is prosperity!" Dr. Stan boldly teaches the truth of God's Word on this very crucial topic. This book will answer many questions and give practical applications from the Word of God that will lead you to walk in prosperity. It is filled with Biblical understanding and in-depth information of the will of God to bless and prosper you!

Dr. Stan's humorous style of writing makes this book an easy read without distorting the facts. The creativity of this presentation of Biblical information gives us a fresh look at the path to prosperity that we must choose to take. I believe that if you take your Bible and notebook, sit down and meditate upon the richness of this book, you will find that every misconception on prosperity is shattered and a new, fresh insight is released because truly, *"God's will is prosperity"*

Pastor Allan Kiuna
Senior Pastor,
Jubilee Christian Church, Nairobi, Kenya

ENDORSEMENT

───∞∞∞───

This book is a powerful tool which will equip the unenlightened, uninformed and *ignorant* (Hosea 4:6) of their God-given right and supply the necessary information to access greater levels of wealth and prosperity as outlined in The Word of God.

God's will still is Prosperity clearly illustrates many truths and presents them in an informed, readable and enjoyable manner and mode. The content, while simple to grasp, also offers well-selected, thought provoking, varied and academic insights.

The *Gospel of prosperity* is one that has been preached with great gusto over the last decade. Dr Stan's approach and coverage of this subject is carefully paced, persuasive, pleasant and well packaged. This is a timeless study which I believe will travel the corridors of time effortlessly while emerging to radiate new light on this vast area. Dr Stan's writing and research is rich in its content, deep in its impact and intellectual, but yet simple in its approach. Well done Dr. Stan.

I believe that every reader who may be faced with an undesirable economic situation, especially in light of the current global crisis, will feel sufficiently impressed after reading this book, to ask the rhetorical question...."*What Credit Crunch? God's Will still is Prosperity*!

Pastor Avis Darlymple
Senior Pastor
Word of life community church, London, UK

ENDORSEMENT

Prosperity is a very vital doctrine of the Christian faith that Dr. Stan will help you de-mystify. Dr. Stan is more that just a friend to me. He is a respected and anointed Minister of our day. A true son of Africa! His teachings are inspiring and building the body of Christ, bringing her to a place of maturity and responsibility.

In endorsing and recommending this book to you, let me remind you the Gospel of John talks of how the Life that was in Christ was the light of men. Again, in the book of Matthew, Jesus says *'Ye are the light of the world'*.

As Dr. Stan takes you through this journey, let the Light of Christ in your life grow brighter as you become a brighter light for men! Open your heart and let the revelation of prosperity inscribed in this book be yours to walk in. let the Wisdom revealed in this book become a reality in your life! Enjoy *"God's will is Prosperity!"*

Pastor George Mathu
Senior Pastor,
Eagle's Faith Christian Centre, Nairobi, Kenya

ENDORSEMENT

If you prayerfully read this book **"God's will *still* is prosperity"** by Dr. Stan Wangenye, you will be greatly enlightened concerning this crucial topic of prosperity. As you read, purpose to put these principles into practice and never let them slip away from your life. The Bible in Hosea Chapter four and verse six gives us 3 major reasons why God's people suffer destruction in any area of their lives. Many are grappling with poverty and not benefiting from God's plan to prosper them, because of these 3 reasons. The **first** reason is a *lack of knowledge*. The **second** is *rebellion or disobedience* to God's will and the **third** reason God's people suffer destruction is *forgetfulness*. Let this book enrich your knowledge, correct the areas of your life where you have been disobedient to God's principles of prosperity and constantly remind you of God's amazing plan to bless you in all things.

The Bible in James Chapter one informs us that it's the doers not just the hearers [or readers] of God's Word who are blessed. The word blessed means to be *empowered to prosper!* Go into your world and do these things and watch God transform your life from faith to faith, strength to strength and glory to glory.

Pastor Kamau Karanja
Senior Pastor,
Greater Glory Church, Nairobi, Kenya

FORWARD

I'm so glad you have this book in your hands. Surely it's by design that at this very critical time globally, you have the opportunity to open your heart and mind to "new things" the Lord will show you in *God's Will Is Still Prosperity*. He will use this book to prepare and position you to move through the days ahead in victory, strength, and blessing.

I've been privileged to know Dr. Stan Wangenye for many years. I remember his joy and enthusiasm as a student in Bible school. Those were the years when he was learning many new Bible truths, and the Lord was forming his faith for ministry. I've seen his struggles, and I've rejoiced to see him **"press on to know the Lord"** in spite of those difficulties. His is a faith tried by fire, and I'm so glad he's chosen to share many of the lessons he's learned with us in this book.

As you read and glean from the truths Dr. Stan reveals in chapter after chapter, you will see that the financial crisis the world is experiencing need not be our crisis. Before you even read the first chapter, begin to say in your heart, "I am in this world, but I am not of this world. Greater is

He who is within me, than he who is in this world." Let faith rise up in your heart to receive from God!

I'm impressed to say to you: as you incorporate this revelation into your life and as you walk in it faithfully, you are going to experience *unusual* breakthroughs in the months ahead. Some will be amazing. Some will be quieter than others. Some will involve a great release. But all will be for God's glory. You will have the testimony that in spite of all that is happening on the world's stage, *God's Will Is Still Prosperity*!

Pastor Carla Porter
Senior Pastor
Victory Faith Church, Nairobi, Kenya

PROLOGUE

⸺∞⸺

In the midst of tumultuous times in the Global Financial Markets, Believers in Christ must have a clear revelation of God's Will for their lives! The body of Christ is *not* just going to survive the credit crunch and global down - turn the world is facing! No *Sir*! The Church is going to *arise* and *shine* in this hour and, like Winston Churchill once said, this *could* be our finest hour! How is the church going to shine? By understanding *and* doing the Will of GOD!

God's Will for every one of us is prosperity! The most basic and fundamental understanding the Church must be aware of, is the fact that God *is* a good God! Yes, He *is*! The sum total of Who God is, *is* GOOD! All that He desires for His people is that we succeed in *absolutely* everything we do! It never was, nor will it ever be, His plan, intent, design or purpose for His people to fail! However, His people, through a lack of knowledge, fail in life and end up being the tail and not the head!

Through the knowledge *and the application* of God's Word, we *can* be *all* that He has purposed for us to be! We *can* have *all* that He has provided for us through Jesus Christ, our Lord!

As we establish in this book that God's Will for us *still* is prosperity, make the quality decision to be all God created you to be, have all God created you to have. Whatever you may be facing in life, whatever the Global Financial situation maybe right now, '*God's Will for you still is prosperity!* – Wangenye

SECTION 1

Prosperity
For
The whole man

"And God said; let us make man in
Our image, after our likeness: and
let them have dominion…"
Genesis 1:26(a)

⸺⸺

Chapter One

What is
Prosperity?

"Life is a journey.
Set yourself to enjoy the Ride!"
Wangenye

—∞∞∞—

Beloved, I wish above all things that thou mayest prosperity and be in health, even as thy soul prospereth. 3John 2

God's will is prosperity! I'd like to draw your attention to the verse of Scripture quoted above. In it, we note that God states His wishes or Will concerning you and me! Over and above all other things, He wishes *'that we may prosper and be in health, even as our soul prospers'*! That word 'wish' is translated from the Greek word: *'uchomai'* (yoo'-khom-ahee) which means; "to wish; to pray to God, to will".

When God says He wishes (prays or wills) above *all* things that I may prosper, I believe Him! Since He is God, His priorities are Divine! What I read Him telling me is that His priority for me, above all things, is that I prosper!

Watch this.

My people are destroyed for lack of knowledge: because thou hast rejected knowledge, I will also reject thee, that thou shalt be no priest to me: seeing thou hast forgotten the law of thy God, I will also forget thy children. Hosea 4:6

Due to a lack of knowledge, God's people are destroyed! It's not because the devil is big, bad and powerful, that God's people are destroyed! No sir! It's just because they lack knowledge of God's Will for their lives!

Look at this. On the one hand, there is this part of the body of Christ who are misinformed regarding prosperity!

27

They have such misconceptions of the prosperity message that, whenever somebody mentions the word 'prosperity', visions of mountains of stacks of money immediately appears in their minds! Prosperity does not mean truckloads of money, pressed down, shaken together and running over! Hear me, now!!

Prosperity *does* include money, but it's *definitely* not *just* about money! God is so much bigger than money! In fact, money is but just *one* dimension of the prosperity message, as we shall see later on in this book!

And then, on the other hand, there is this other part of the body of Christ who hate, detest, talk bad about the prosperity message, again, as a result of misinformation! *Yet, this bunch will dutifully trot to work every working day of their lives, trying to earn money and get wealthy!* Hello! Are they coming or going?!!

How about this other group in the church who are possessed by a phobia of becoming prosperous! In their eyes, it seems that if a believer prospers financially, he or she is looked upon as if he or she has sinned in getting wealthy!

satan has, for too long, used ignorance in the church concerning prosperity to keep the church incapacitated in carrying out the great commission of reaching the world with the Gospel of Jesus Christ. This state of affairs has been made worse by religious teachings that *'poverty is a blessing'* since, say they, Jesus said that a rich man *'could not'* enter into the kingdom of God! Bah!!

You need to read the text in context otherwise you'll end up with a pretext!

Let us take a moment and read this particular Scripture so often misquoted.

And when he was gone forth into the way, there came one running, and kneeled to him, and asked him, Good Master, what shall I do that I may inherit eternal life? And Jesus said unto him, Why callest thou me good? there is none good but one, that is, God. Thou knowest the commandments, Do not commit adultery, Do not kill, Do not steal, Do not bear false witness, Defraud not, Honour thy father and mother. And he answered and said unto him, Master, all these have I observed from my youth. Then Jesus beholding him loved him, and said unto him, One thing thou lackest: go thy way, sell what-soever thou hast, and give to the poor, and thou shalt have treasure in heaven: and come, take up the cross, and follow me. And he was sad at that saying, and went away grieved: for he had great posses-sions. And Jesus looked round about, and saith unto his disciples, How hardly shall they that have riches enter into the kingdom of God! And the disciples were astonished at his words. But Jesus answereth again, and saith unto them, Children, how hard is it for them that trust in riches to enter into the kingdom of God! It is easier for a camel to go through the eye of a needle, than for a rich man to enter into the kingdom of God. And they were astonished out of measure, saying among themselves, Who then can be saved? Mark 10:17-26

If you'll notice, the only reason Jesus said it would be difficult for a rich man to enter into the kingdom of God is because the rich young ruler wouldn't let go of his money for nothing! It's like he was married to his money!! In his case, money had him, instead of him having money! God has nothing against you having money but He has everything against money having you! The disciples were utterly astonished by this teaching, wondering amongst themselves, '*who then can be saved?*'

I ask you, why would they ask such a question if they had been poor? They should have had absolutely no reason to be concerned, had they been poor! Had poverty been the criteria used to enter into heaven, they should have shouted for joy! Instead, they started to fret about '*rich men not entering heaven*'! They must have been rich! Had they been poor, they should have been rejoicing that they *were* poor and therefore qualified to enter into the kingdom of God! It must mean the disciples were loaded with the stuff!!

And Jesus confirms the above thought 3 verses later!

Watch!

> *And Jesus answered and said, Verily I say unto you, There is no man that hath left house, or brethren, or sisters, or father, or mother, or wife, or children, or lands, for my sake, and the gospel's, But he shall receive an hundredfold now in this time, houses, and brethren, and sisters, and mothers, and children, and lands, with persecutions; and in the world to come eternal life.* Mark 10: 29-30

The rich young ruler should have waited to hear Jesus respond to the *'who can be saved'* question! He missed it by *3* verses! Whatever you give up for the Kingdom of God, you will be given back a hundredfold now, *in this time*! And life eternal in the next! This is what Jesus said! He did not want the rich young ruler to become poor after giving up all his possessions! On the contrary, Jesus wanted the rich young ruler to receive a hundredfold return on *all* he was asked to give away! Jesus was *not* telling him to become poorer but richer! Amen!

Now then, when the church finally started to get the revelation of the prosperity message, some in the Christian circles took it from one ditch right into the other! They abused it, misused it and took advantage of a God-given principle to feed their greed. The fact that some don't believe or teach the prosperity message at all does not invalidate the message! Neither is the misapplication or abuse of the prosperity message by some, mean that we shouldn't believe *and* apply the real thing! The existence of counterfeit money does not invalidate the real thing!! It's time this message was taught and applied in a balanced manner! *It worketh*!

And so, to wash away all misconceptions and misunder-standings concerning the prosperity message from our minds, we are going to look at the root Greek and Hebrew words so as to fully understand that it's God's will for the body of Christ to prosper.

Come with me, first, to the Epistle of John.

> *Beloved, I wish above all things that thou mayest prosper and be in health, even as thy soul prospereth.* 3 John 2

Let us look at the definition of the word 'prosper'. In the above scripture, it is defined from the Greek word; *'euodoo'* (yoo-od-o'-o) which means; "to help on the road, succeed in reaching; to succeed in business affairs, to have a prosperous journey".

Prosperity then, going by the Greek rendition of the word, is more than having so much money; it's coming out of our ears! In fact, money is not even mentioned in this definition! Life is not *just* about money! God is more than money and He is more interested in our state than our estate or financial status! He is very interested in our welfare! Where money is required, money will be made available. Where favor is all you need, favor will be made available. Living in divine health means you do not need to use your money paying medical bills! Hello, somebody!

So, we see that God wishes us to have help on the road of life, succeed in reaching our destination, and have a good and prosperous journey in life! Somebody once said that life is a journey. Set yourself to enjoy the ride!

> *I will lift up mine eyes unto the hills, from whence cometh my help. My help cometh from the LORD, which made heaven and earth.* Psalm 121:1- 2

Thank God my help comes from a source far more superior than money! Money can only do so much! There are situations that we face in life that no amount of money can solve. There are sicknesses that money cannot buy prescriptions for. There are doors that the favor of the Lord will open for you that no amount of money can. There is a level of peace of mind that driving the top-of-the line Mercedes Benz will not guarantee! There is a sense of well being that cannot be guaranteed by the size of your home, no matter which side of the tracks it is located! A mansion in the best part of the French Riviera or a nice Spanish villa some place in Hollywood is no guarantee for trouble-free living! God alone is our safe hiding-place, the sure guarantee of our well-being, dead or alive! O Glory Hallelujah!

Mind you! I have no objection to enjoying material prosperity gained in a Godly fashion! What I am saying, is that, I would rather have Jesus, than silver or gold as my source of confidence! I join the Psalmist in making my bold confession; *"My help comes from the Lord!"*

> *Blessed is the man that walketh not in the counsel of the ungodly, nor standeth in the way of sinners, nor sitteth in the seat of the scornful. But his delight is in the law of the LORD; and in his law doth he meditate day and night. And he shall be like a tree planted by the rivers of water, that bringeth forth his fruit in his season; his leaf also shall not wither; and whatsoever he doeth shall prosper. Psalm 1:1-3*

Let us now look at the definition of the word; 'prosper' from the Scripture quoted above. It is defined from the

Hebrew word; tsalach (tsaw-lakh' or tsaw-lay'-akh) which means; "to push forward, to break out, to come mightily, to go over, to be good, to be meet, to be profitable".

This definition really excites me!! God's will for you and me is, whatsoever we do, we receive His help to 'push' us forward so as 'to break out' of all our limitations! We are to 'come mightily' to our destiny, and realize our intended purpose! Whatever we do, God desires it 'to be good' (and not bad!), for it to 'go over' (and never under!), for it 'to be meet and acceptable' (and never unacceptable) and for it to always be 'profitable' (and not a loss-plagued enterprise!)

It is time the body of Christ really got the revelation that God does want us to succeed in everything we do! His desire is that, as we live our lives by the standard of His Word, we are to prosper in everything we do! The time to break out of our limitations is now! The time to push forward is now! The time to excel is now! The day of the mediocre church is over! In fact, it never was God's will for the church to be mediocre! The church simply didn't have the revelation that God's will was, and still is, and always will be, prosperity! O Praise the Lord!

We are to be good and succeed in everything we do. We are to be meet and acceptable in whatever we do. We are to be profitable in everything we set our hands to do! The church is meant to be the most prosperous entity on earth! We are meant to be the most sought-after people on the planet! Everything we do should go over and never under! Financial institutions are meant to be vying for our business, to the point of them fighting each other! This is because our businesses are so very good and sound that, having us as their clients would enhance their corporate image and business no end! Can this really be possible? Yes it can!! God's will for us is prosperity! Success beyond our wildest imagination!

Since I live in 'gud ole' England, I cannot but look up the word in the 'gud ole' dictionary!

The word 'prosper', as defined by the English dictionary, means; 'to help on one's way, to thrive, to turn out well, to experience favorable circumstances'. It is God's will that we have help on our way. Look at what the Psalmist says about this.

> *God is our refuge and strength, a very present help in trouble. Therefore will not we fear, though the earth be removed, and though the mountains be carried into the midst of the sea; Though the waters thereof roar and be troubled, though the mountains shake with the swelling thereof. Selah.* Psalm 46:1-3

God not only sends us help but He *Himself* is our help, to help *us* on our way! Even though trouble comes, God is our refuge and a very present help in trouble!! God's people are never without help! He promised He'll never leave us nor forsake us! Whatever your situation is, God is a very present help in trouble!

God's people are meant *to thrive* wherever they are. Whatever your occupation, God's will is that you thrive, flourish and bloom! Since we have the life of God dwelling within us, we should be able to give life to everything we touch! Businesses belonging to members of the body of Christ ought to be thriving to the point of attracting comment from the world! Everything we do should be *turning out very, very well*! We should be, and actually *need* to be, experiencing very favorable circumstances in everything we do!

Oh, but Dr. Stan, do you not see the status of our country's economy? Do you not know that business is slow and the money markets are in a depression? Have you not heard of the credit crunch and the global financial downturn?

Hey! Listen!! Our *turning out well* is not governed by the status of the world's economy! We are in covenant with the God of heaven! Heaven's economy is always robust!! We have the provision from God, of prospering even when our country's economy is in a depression! Isaac experienced this when he sowed and reaped a hundredfold return in a time the country was experiencing a famine. *(Genesis 26:12)* Since God is no respecter of persons, He will do the same for us! And more, too, seeing we have a better covenant that is established on better promises!! *(Hebrews 8:6)*

Oh, but Dr. Stan, what about the wicked who prosper and don't seem to have any problems? Sounds to me like the same thing Jeremiah had a problem with. Notice what he said:

> *Righteous art thou, O LORD, when I plead with thee: yet let me talk with thee of thy judgments: Wherefore doth the way of the wicked prosper? wherefore are all they happy that deal very treacherously?* Jeremiah 12:1

Have you ever felt like talking to God like Jeremiah did? Or have you actually done it? Tell the truth, now! I know I have. Have you ever been obedient to God concerning finances and it seemed the moment you paid your tithes, all 'hell' broke lose in your finances? And to add insult to injury, there is this wicked neighbor of yours who seemed to 'prosper' even more in his wickedness! And sometimes he looked like he was prospering at your expense! If you ever have, or you are in this kind of situation, take heart! You are not the first and neither will you be the last to experience this! David also took it up with God about it, so let's learn from him through the following Psalm.

Fret not thyself because of evildoers, neither be thou envious against the workers of iniquity. For they shall soon be cut down like the grass, and wither as the green herb. Mark the perfect man, and behold the upright: for the end of that man is peace. Psalm 37:1-2, 37

The wicked will not turn out well, if they remain wicked. Going to hell is definitely not turning out well or having a good journey. The wicked person's destination will be 'one hell of a hot place'! Envy not the wicked and his prosperity since it is not real prosperity! Rejoice, though, for your end is peace!

Chapter two

Spiritual prosperity

"Gaining the world
And losing your soul
Is a no-brainer!"
Wangenye

The first, most important area God has provided prosperity for man is the area of spiritual prosperity. In the creational Text, God created man in His own image and likeness. Look at the following verse.

And God said, Let us make man in our image, after our likeness: and let them have dominion over the fish of the sea, and over the fowl of the air, and over the cattle, and over all the earth, and over every creeping thing that creepeth upon the earth. Genesis 1:26

Here, we see God, Jehovah *Elohiym*, the Almighty Creator, holding a consultative meeting with God His Son and God His Spirit. The agenda on that day's meeting was: *"Let us make man in our image, after our likeness:"* First of all, it may come as a shock to some that God actually consults and seeks advice! Yes, He does!

By the very wording of the above Scripture, we hear God calling the other two Beings of the Holy Trinity and saying, *"let us"* and, by implication, opens up His Agenda to suggestions from the other two Beings in His Trinity. *'Let us'* is tantamount to saying; 'what do you think?' or 'I need your agreement and participation in this'. Whenever we say to somebody, 'let us do such and such', we are, by implication, inviting three kinds of responses;

One:	Yes, let's do it as you have suggested!
Two:	Could we change detail so and so before implementing the suggestion?
Three:	No, I don't think that is a good idea at all and I really don't want to be part of it.

Evidently, God takes counsel and is open to suggestions from Himself! See what Paul says about this.

In whom also we have obtained an inheritance, being predestinated according to the purpose of him who worketh all things after the counsel of his own will: Ephesians 1:11

God works! This might be a revelation to some, but you just heard the truth! For those who might think they are redeemed from working, please take note that God *actually* works! And as the children of our heavenly Father, we should emulate Him by getting some work done!

Please notice here also, that He works *all* things after the counsel of His own will! To me, that is saying that, whenever God gets ready to work something, He pulls out a copy of His Will, (also known as the Testaments, also known as the Word of God, also known as the Bible) and takes counsel from it! Is it any wonder, therefore, that He has magnified His Word above all His Name? (*Psalm 138:2*) And since God works after the counsel of His own Will, how much more shouldn't *we* seek the counsel of His Will?

Now then, we have seen that God has created us in His image and likeness. Do you mean to tell me that man *physically* looks like God? Not necessarily! From what I can see in Scripture, God does *not* have a body (except the body of Christ, also known as the church of God)! The Bible says that God is Spirit!! And Jesus said that Spirits do not have flesh and bones (bodies)! Let us read it.

God is a Spirit: and they that worship him must worship him in spirit and in truth. John 4:24

Behold my hands and my feet, that it is I myself: handle me, and see; for a spirit hath not flesh and bones, as ye see me have. Luke 24:39

The word *'flesh'* in Luke 24:39 is translated from Greek word: *"sarx"*. One of its meaning, is, "the body (as opposed to the soul (or spirit), or as the symbol of what is external,". Remember what happened after Adam and Eve ate of the forbidden fruit? The Bible says they *heard* the voice of the Lord *walking* in the garden and they hid themselves. In fact, let us go ahead and read it.

And they heard the voice of the LORD God walking in the garden in the cool of the day: and Adam and his wife hid themselves from the presence of the LORD God amongst the trees of the garden. And the LORD God called unto Adam, and said unto him, Where art thou? And he said, I heard thy voice in the garden, and I was afraid, because I was naked; and I hid myself. Genesis 3:8-10

Notice here the Bible does not say they *saw* Him walking in the garden in the cool of the day! They *heard* His voice *walking!* This is because you can *hear* the Spirit but you can't *see* Him. You will, however, see His manifestation and work!

We can therefore suggest, going by what the Bible is saying here, that God is a Spirit without a body (except the body of Christ). And He made us in His own image.

Our spirits are created to look just like His! And His Spirit is prosperous! Never at any time will He ever be broke! His Spirit is always thriving, having a good journey and turning out well! Our spirits, in creation, were prosperous, just like His Spirit! But something happened in the Garden of Eden that caused our spirit to go bankrupt! So, what happened?

And the LORD God commanded the man, saying, Of every tree of the garden thou mayest freely eat: But of the tree of the knowledge of good and evil, thou shalt not eat of it: for in the day that thou eatest thereof thou shalt surely die. Genesis 2:16, 17

And when the woman saw that the tree was good for food, and that it was pleasant to the eyes, and a tree to be desired to make one wise, she took of the fruit thereof, and did eat, and gave also unto her husband with her; and he did eat. Genesis 3:6

And they heard the voice of the LORD God walking in the garden in the cool of the day: and Adam and his wife hid themselves from the presence of the LORD God amongst the trees of the garden. Genesis 3:8

We see in the above Scriptures, how God *freely* gave *everything* that was in the Garden of Eden to Adam, with one exception: the tree of the knowledge of good and evil. Just *one* commandment and Adam would have remained spiritually prosperous for eternity!! But did he obey it? Noooooo! Greed and lust got the better of him and he disobeyed God!

Men, before you cop out with *"it's the woman You gave me"* line, please notice that Adam was with her all the time! The Bible says that Eve gave unto her husband *with her* and he did eat. The man had been party to the mutiny all along! As soon as that rebellion took place, the image of God, in the form of His Spirit, departed from them and they realized they were naked!

And as was His custom, God comes in to fellowship with Adam and Eve in the cool of the day and alas!, they were hiding! His image in and on them had departed and they had lost their spiritual prosperity! God, being merciful and just, clothed them with animal skins and moved them out of the garden, lest they eat of the tree of life and live eternally in a state of sin!

But that is not where the story ends because God *never* gives up on His dreams! His dream and vision for man is for man to be a spiritually prosperous being! God created man spiritually prosperous so that they two can commune together for eternity! This state of righteousness or right standing with God is what I call 'spiritual prosperity'! And God's plans and purposes are eternal! He stayed true to His promise of sending a Savior, who would 'crush' the serpent's head. Through this Savior, Jesus Christ, we have regained the spiritual prosperity that was lost in the garden! Look at the following Scriptures.

For God so loved the world, that he gave his only begotten Son, that whosoever believeth in him should not perish, but have everlasting life. John 3:16

...... For this purpose the Son of God was manifested, that he might destroy the works of the devil. 1John 3:8(b)

Who hath delivered us from the power of darkness, and hath translated us into the kingdom of his dear Son: In whom we have redemption through his blood, even the forgiveness of sins: Col 1:13, 14

Therefore if any man be in Christ, he is a new creature: old things are passed away; behold, all things are become new. And all things are of God, who hath reconciled us to himself by Jesus Christ, and hath given to us the ministry of reconciliation; 2 Cor 5:17,18

For the law of the Spirit of life in Christ Jesus hath made me free from the law of sin and death. Romans 8:2

What Adam lost in the Garden of Eden, Jesus Christ paid the ultimate price to get it back! After striping the devil of what rightfully belonged to us, He *now* offers it to all who will come to God through Him! We *now* have the availability of spiritual prosperity through Jesus Christ! By being born again, man is translated from the kingdom of satan to the kingdom of God's dear Son, Jesus Christ! The law of sin and death is broken from his life and he becomes a new creation in God! His spiritual destination is no longer hell, but heaven! He now is thriving and will turn out well! I would say going to heaven is turning out very well indeed!

Jesus had this to say about owning earthly wealth and still go to hell:

For what is a man profited, if he shall gain the whole world, and lose his own soul? or what shall a man give in exchange for his soul? Matthew 16:26

Jesus is showing us, in the above Scriptures, that spiritual prosperity is of a higher dimension and importance than material prosperity! This does not mean we don't *need* material prosperity, but what it does say is that material prosperity is not the most important aspect of prosperity! We will look at material prosperity later but, we need to see everything in its proper perspective. We need to keep the prosperity message well balanced and in the middle of the road!

You may be reading this book and you are still not sure of your eternal destiny. Consider what Jesus said in the verse we have just read. You might consider yourself financially well off. How are you, then, spiritually? Without Jesus Christ as your Saviour, things, from a spiritual stand point, do not look so good for you! If this is your status, all is not lost! There is a prayer at the end of this book, which I would encourage you to pray right away. Do not put it off till you finish the book! Put a book-mark or your finger here and turn to page 179. It has a heading *"Prayer for salvation and the baptism in the Holy Spirit"*. Go ahead and pray this prayer and I guarantee you, based on the Word of God, your end will turn out well! Going to heaven is definitely turning out well! Thank God for His Provision of spiritual prosperity!!

Chapter three

Mental prosperity

"O, precious, precious peace!
How amiable are thy courts!
How desirable they are
to me!"

Wangenye

It may come as a surprise to some that there is such a thing as 'mental prosperity'. Remember our definitions from chapter one of the word 'prosperity'. We need to understand that God has made provision for us to enjoy peace of mind! Our mental status should be thriving, turning out well and enjoying favorable circumstances. The Bible has numerous references of God's provision for our peace. For the purpose of our study, we will mention but a few.

For unto us a child is born, unto us a son is given: and the government shall be upon his shoulder: and his name shall be called Wonderful, Counsellor, The mighty God, The everlasting Father, The Prince of Peace. Of the increase of his government and peace there shall be no end, upon the throne of David, and upon his kingdom, to order it, and to establish it with judgment and with justice from henceforth even for ever. The zeal of the LORD of hosts will perform this. Isaiah 9:6, 7(a)

Thou wilt keep him in perfect peace, whose mind is stayed on thee: because he trusteth in thee.... LORD, thou wilt ordain peace for us: for thou also hast wrought all our works in us. Isaiah 26:3, 12

And the peace of God, which passeth all understanding, shall keep your hearts and minds through Christ Jesus. Philippians 4:7

God so loved the world that He gave His only begotten son, who paid the price for our redemption: spirit, soul and body. Jesus came to us as the Prince of Peace! The verse we've just read in Isaiah 9:7 states that *'of the increase of His government and peace, there shall be no end'*.

When we receive Jesus as our Lord and Saviour, we experience an aspect of peace we never knew before! We get this sense of well being, knowing that we are reconciled with our Maker! That is a very peaceful thought and fact! In fact, Jesus Christ categorically states that He actually gave us His peace, peace like He has it! Let's read it.

> *Peace I leave with you, my peace I give unto you: not as the world giveth, give I unto you. Let not your heart be troubled, neither let it be afraid.* John 14:27

It is a fact, therefore, that the peace that Jesus Christ gives us, ought to be *in* us! Why is it, then, that so many in the body Christ do not enjoy this peace? Our answer is in the second Scripture we quoted above from the book of Isaiah.

God will keep us in perfect peace when we keep our minds on Him and His word! We cannot let our minds focus and dwell on the negative forces of the world and then expect to walk in the peace of God! We must let our thoughts be centred on God and His Word for us to enjoy the God-Kind of peace! Keep your mind on the Promise and not on the problem! The solution to your problem is in the Promise! Keep your mind on the promises of God so as to be able to see the solution to your problem! Look at what Peter says about our peace:

Grace and peace be multiplied unto you through the knowledge of God, and of Jesus our Lord, 2 Peter 1:2

Not only can we have the peace of God, but we can *actually* have that peace *multiplied* unto us! Boy! I really like this one!

Remember we read in Isaiah 9:7 that '*the increase of His government and of peace there shall be no end*'? Whatever amount of peace you may be walking in right now; there is God-given possibility for having it multiplied! How? '*Through the knowledge of God, our heavenly Father, and of Jesus Christ, our Lord*'. How does one know God? The primary avenue of knowing God is through His word! The more revelation of God you get, the greater the availability of God's peace!!

And the peace of God, which passeth all under-standing, shall keep your hearts and minds through Christ Jesus. Philippians 4:7

This is a promise we really need to get a hold of. The word 'keep' is translated from the Greek word, *'phroureo'* (froo-reh'-o) which means; "to be a watcher in the advance, to mount guard as a sentinel, to post spies at gates; to hem in, protect, to garrison."

God's peace will '*mount guard, hem in, protect and garrison our minds through Christ Jesus!* I would say no enemy is going to get through that!!

So, mental prosperity *is* provided for in God. Why is peace so vital to the body of Christ? Without it, you can't possibly hear God accurately! When you are flustered, fretful, worried and fearful, you more often than not make decisions based on these emotions! God leads us in peace and our decisions need to be made in an atmosphere of mental peace. The reason why I say mental peace is because circumstances can be tumultuous around you but your mental state can be peaceful. Remember Peter hearing Jesus say *'come'* in the middle of a storm? He made a decision to go to Jesus, disregarding the circumstances around him. He walked on water to go to Jesus and only began to sink when he shifted his focus from the Word Jesus spoke to him and fixed it on the storm around him!(Matthew 14:29-30) The storm can be all *around* you but it does not have to be *in* you!

Look at the following verse of scripture

> *And let the peace of God rule in your hearts, to which also ye are called in one body; and be ye, thankful.* Colossians 3:15

Notice here that the peace of God is meant to rule our heart. That word, 'rule' is translated from Greek word, *'brabeuo'* (brab-yoo'-o) which means, "to arbitrate, to govern". The peace of God is to 'arbitrate and govern our hearts!' That word 'heart' is translated from the Greek word, *'kardia'* (kar-dee'-ah) which figuratively means, "the thoughts or feeling". So we see that our thoughts and feeling are to be governed by peace! The Amplified version of the Bible says that *'the peace of God is to act as umpire continually in your hearts, deciding and settling with finality all questions that arise in your minds'*. Given that God has so emphatically said that we are to have His peace, we need to understand the enemies of His peace.

ENEMIES OF PEACE

1.   The devil-kind of fear

The first negative spirit that tries to rob us of our peace is fear from satan. The reason why I say fear from satan is because the Bible *does* teaches us to walk in the fear of the Lord. To differentiate one fear from the other, I will call one the God-kind of fear and the other, the devil-kind of fear.

Let us start with the devil-kind of fear. Watch what the following scripture says.

For God hath not given us the spirit of fear; but of power, and of love, and of a sound mind. 2 Timothy 1:7

The devil-kind of fear is not of God and God has not given us *this* spirit of fear. The dictionary defines this kind of fear as "a painful emotion excited by danger; an apprehension of danger or pain; an alarm". The devil-kind of fear is a spirit that attacks our emotions with apprehensions of danger! The danger may not be there yet, but only the *apprehension* or suspicion of it! What the spirit of fear does, is that it takes that apprehension or suspicion and causes one to fear! This kind of fear causes the one fearing to be terrified and God *definitely* is not a terrorist!

Notice here, also, that God is saying He has not given us the spirit of fear! If God is not the one giving the spirit of fear, then it must be the devil dishing it out! And you don't have to partake of the devil's dish, either! Let's see what is God's antidote for the devil-kind of fear.

There is no fear in love; but perfect love casteth out fear: because fear hath torment. He that feareth is not made perfect in love. 1 John 4:18

An increase in your faith level is important but it *will not* necessarily solve the fear issue!

Notice the Scripture does not say that perfect *faith* casteth out fear. It says perfect *love* casteth out fear. Even faith must work by love. *(Galatians 5:6)* We cast out the lesser by the greater and the greatest of faith, hope and love *is* love! *(1 Corinthians 13:13)*

Neither is the answer to the devil-kind of fear lie in maximum-security arrangements for your home! Please!! Be prudent and do what you've got to do where your security arrangements are concerned. It's important to secure yourself and yours! However, these security arrangements do not guarantee immunity from fear! You might keep the bugler off your premises but the fear of the bugler *cannot* be kept out with steel gates and high fences!

Neither is the answer in alcohol or drugs, which only serves to deceive the one taking them! Taking drugs to escape reality *does not* take you *out* of reality! The drugs only deceive you that you *are* out of it! You'll wake up in the morning, out of pocket financially, with a massive hung over and in jail! You'll wake up just in time to realise the *'same old, same old'* is still the *'same old, same old'*.

The solution to the devil-kind of fear *is* God's love. We need to understand that the weapons that defeat spiritual forces of wickedness, such as fear, are not carnal! We deal with these wicked spirits with Godly, spiritual force! We address the devil-kind of fear (which is an evil spirit) with the God-kind of love (which is a Godly spiritual force)!

Having said that, let us now look at what the Bible *does* teach about the fear of the Lord.

There are numerous reference made in the Bible regarding the fear of the Lord, so let us confine ourselves to a few of them.

The fear of the LORD is the beginning of knowl-edge: but fools despise wisdom and instruction. Proverbs 1:7

Then shall they call upon me, but I will not answer; they shall seek me early, but they shall not find me: For that they hated knowledge, and did not choose the fear of the LORD: Proverbs 1:28, 29

The fear of the LORD is to hate evil: pride, and arrogancy, and the evil way, and the froward mouth, do I hate. Proverbs 8:13

In the fear of the LORD is strong confidence: and his children shall have a place of refuge. The fear of the LORD is a fountain of life, to depart from the snares of death. Proverbs 14:26,27

Notice, here, that the fear of the Lord is the beginning of Knowledge. The word, *'fear'* in the above scripture is defined from the Hebrew word, *'yir'ah'*. One of its meaning is, 'moral reverence'. It also means "to have great respect for God, to stand in awe of Him". This Godly fear is not like the devil-kind of terror! No Sir! It is to revere God.

The God-kind of fear is to hate evil! (And to depart from it, I might add.) To choose the fear of the Lord positions us to seek God and finding Him, calling on Him and Him answering us! That is the message we get from Proverbs 1:28, 29.To choose the fear of the Lord also gives us strong confidence when approaching the Lord. Proverbs 14:27 states that this *'fear of the lord is a fountain of life and keeps us from the snares of death'*. These snares are sins whose wages is death. (Romans 6:23) It is therefore highly recommended that we choose the God-kind of fear and refuse, renounce and fight against the devil-kind of fear!

2. Anxiety

The other negative spirit we want to deal with is anxiety. A large portion of the body of Christ *really* struggle with this one.

Look at what God says is to be our state of mind where anxiety is concerned.

*Be careful for nothing; but in every thing by prayer
and supplication with thanksgiving let your requests
be made known unto God.* Philippians 4:6

The word 'careful' is translated from the Greek word,
'*merimnao*' (mer-im-nah'-o), which means; "to be anxious
about, to be or have care, to take thought".

Notice here, then, that God is telling us to be anxious
or take thought for nothing! Yet how many believers do
exactly the opposite! They are anxious about *everything!*
The kids are on drugs, the bills are pilling up, the credit
crunch will munch me, there is no food in the house,
Osama is on the prowl, the end of the world is at hand, the
cat is sick, the dog has fleas, and just about everything else
under the sun!

Hey! Listen! God has said for us to be anxious for nothing!
Nothing means *nothing!* Osama or no Osama, Jesus Christ
is Lord! God is *still* on the throne and He is not shaking
in His boots wondering what He is going to do about the
dreaded Osama of the day! Can you image God shaking
and rocking on His throne, biting His nails and worried sick
about the 'Osamas' who are out to get you!? Ridiculous
and absolutely out of the question! Jehovah God knows
the end from the beginning! Just because man may be
struggling trying to solve the 'Osama' problems doesn't
mean that God is, too! Nor is the credit crunch *'crunching'*
God's economy!

Notice that God says, in the verse quoted above, for us to
make our requests known unto Him. All we need to do is
ask! O, but brother Stan that sounds so simple. Yes! It's

so simple man has to complicate it! So, brother Stan, have you asked Him about the dreaded Osama? Yes! And what did He say? Shhh… and don't tell anyone! He said Osama ain't god! And not to go stocking up with 3 years' worth of tribulation food, either! If you moved to stock up your pantry motivated by fear, then God didn't lead you to do it because He doesn't lead us by fear! I state once more that God is not a terrorist! Of course, I advocate for wisdom and proper planning which does not replace faith. What I *am* saying is that don't be stampeded into acting out of fear! Jesus Christ is Lord, with or without the bin ladens of our day, credit crunch or no credit crunch, galloping gas prices or no galloping gas prices! Hello, Somebody!

The equation I have for this situation is: bin ladens of today + new millennium + soon return of Christ + same Jehovah God = triumphant church!! Praise the Lord!

Consider the following verse of scripture.

Casting all your care upon him; for he careth for you. 1 Peter 5:7

Therefore I say unto you, Take no thought for your life, what ye shall eat, or what ye shall drink; nor yet for your body, what ye shall put on. Is not the life more than meat, and the body than raiment? Behold the fowls of the air: for they sow not, neither do they reap, nor gather into barns; yet your heavenly Father feedeth them. Are ye not much better than they? Which of you by taking thought can add one cubit unto his stature? And why take ye thought for raiment? Consider the lilies of the field, how they grow; they toil not, neither do they spin: And yet I say unto you, That even Solomon in all his glory was not arrayed like one of these. Wherefore, if God so clothe the grass of the field, which to day is, and to morrow is cast into the oven, shall he not much more clothe you, O ye of little faith? Therefore take no thought, saying, What shall we eat? or, What shall we drink? or, Wherewithal shall we be clothed? (For after all these things do the Gentiles seek:) for your heavenly Father knoweth that ye have need of all these things. But seek ye first the kingdom of God, and his righteousness; and all these things shall be added unto you. Take therefore no thought for the morrow: for the morrow shall take thought for the things of itself. Sufficient unto the day is the evil thereof. Matthew 6:25-34

So instead of being anxious, we should cast all our cares upon Jesus, for He cares for us! This we should do in faith and not in fear of tomorrow. Enjoy the mental prosperity and well being that God has provided for us through Christ Jesus our Lord! Amen!

Chapter Four

Material prosperity

"His Riches bring on
Ease, not *dis*ease"
Wangenye

Material prosperity, which is also known as 'prosperity of the senses', is sub divided into two categories:

a. Health
b. Wealth

For the purpose of our study, we will look at them separately.

HEALTH

God has provided physical well-being for mankind. Through the death, burial and resurrection of our Lord Jesus Christ, everything pertaining to our welfare was accomplished and paid for in full! By the stripes that were laid on Jesus' back, we were provided for with healing.

Let's look at some verses of scripture regarding this.

> *Surely he hath borne our griefs, and carried our sorrows: yet we did esteem him stricken, smitten of God, and afflicted. But he was wounded for our transgressions, he was bruised for our iniquities: the chastisement of our peace was upon him; and with his stripes we are healed.* Isaiah 53:4,5

Surely... God's word is a sure thing! When God adds an affirmative like *'surely'* to His Promise, He really does want us to have absolutely no doubts in our minds as to what His will is! He has not only paid the price for our going to heaven, but also for having a healthy body here on planet earth! With His stripes, we are healed! *'We are healed'* is present continuous tense. As long as there is the possibility of sickness, there is present with us, the cure to that sickness! Praise the Lord!

That word, 'healed' is translated from the Hebrew word, *'rapha'* (raw-faw'), a primary root word meaning: "to mend by stitching, to cure, cause to heal, physician, repair thoroughly, making whole".

No matter how 'fallen apart' you may be feeling, God is able *'stitch'* you back together again! No matter how 'broken down' you may be feeling, He is able to *'mend and repair'* you again! No matter haw 'sick' you may be, He is able *'to cure'* you and cause you to be healed! He is Jehovah Rapha, our physician, who cures us and thoroughly makes us whole!

Oh! By the way, 'by whose stripes' are we talking about? Good question!

Let's look at the following verse of Scripture.

For even hereunto were ye called: because Christ also suffered for us, leaving us an example, that ye should follow his steps: Who did no sin, neither was guile found in his mouth: Who, when he was reviled, reviled not again; when he suffered, he threatened not; but committed himself to him that judgeth righteously: Who his own self bare our sins in his own body on the tree, that we, being dead to sins, should live unto righteousness: by whose stripes ye were healed. 1 Peter 2:21-24

This verse clearly identifies *'by whose stripes'* we were healed! Jesus Christ is Him Name! The Bible states right here that *'He Himself bare our sins on His body on the tree (cross) and by wholes stripes you were healed'*.

Notice here that God says by the stripes that were laid on Jesus, we *were* healed. The tense used here is past tense. What this is saying is that we are not *going* to be healed (future), but rather, we *were* healed! (Past) Healing of our bodies is already a done deal in the realm of the spirit!! But brother Stan, why then do we get sick?

Jesus answered that by saying that satan *'comes only to steal kill and destroy.'* (John 10:10) satan is the one that comes to steal our good health! One characteristic of a thief is that he only steals that which you do have! He doesn't steal that which you don't have! satan tries to steal only what you already possess! Our responsibility is to maintain that which Christ has paid the price for us to have! Fight the good fight of faith and protect your God-given health!

> *Beloved, I wish above all things that thou mayest prosper and be in health, even as thy soul prospereth.* 3 John 1:2

Notice here that God *'wishes (or prays) above all things that we prosper and be in health, even as our souls prospers'*. That word 'health' is translated from the Greek word, *'hugiaino'* (hoog-ee-ah'ee-no) which means, 'to have sound health, to be well in body, to be uncorrupted, be in health, to be safe and sound, to be whole'.

God does not desire any one of His Children to be sick! He is our heavenly Father and desires only good things for His children! Even earthly fathers desire good health for their children. A father who does not wish his children to be in good health must be sick! But notice that we will be in health to the degree our soul prospers. Now, what in the world does that mean?

For us to understand what it means to prosper our soul, we must first understand what the soul is.

The heart of man (not the blood pump!) is made up of two parts: the soul and the spirit. The spirit part is where the Holy Spirit dwells, for those who are born again. The soul part, which we are studying here, is made up of your will, your mind and your emotions. This is your 'decision' department. This is your 'information storage' department. This is your 'emotion department'. The Bible states that the soul and the spirit are so closely knit together that only the Word of God is able to separate them. (Hebrew 4:12)

We need to understand that when we got born again, we didn't get a new brain, will or emotion! The part of our heart that was born again was our spirit part. What is then required for us to do is to *renew* our minds by the Word of God. (Roman 12:2, 3) We are to take our old way of thinking and transform it by the Word of God! Our will is to conform to God's Will and our emotions are to be governed by God's Word. People make wrong decisions, think wrong thoughts and have wrong feelings, because they are drawing from the old, un-renewed mind! Renew the database, man!

This process of replacing our thoughts and old ways of thinking is what is called; 'the prosperity of the soul'. Our will, then lines up with God's will, our minds have the correct data (God's word) and our emotions are governed by God's word!

For as he thinketh in his heart, so is he: ...... Proverbs 23:7 (a)

God gave me a revelation of the above verse as I was meditating on and putting this book together. I had never really understood what He was talking about by the phrase;'*thinketh in his heart*'. How in the world does a '*heart*' think? I thought you used your head for that!

But listen! As I was writing about the components of the heart of man, God just dropped this in my spirit! This is so exciting!! Using the phrase, '*as he thinketh in his heart*', God is talking about the 'heart of man' and not the blood pump! Remember we said that the components of the 'heart of man' are the soul and the spirit. And the soul, we said, is composed of the mind, the will and the emotions.

In other words, God is saying that whatever you think in that part of your 'heart' that does the 'thinking', *that* is what you will become! What you think is governed by what you feed your thoughts with! You either do it from the resources of God's Word or from the resources of the world. If the economist tells you the economy is in a recession and you believe him above the Word of God, you will be in that recession, too! If you feed your thoughts with God's Word, you will sow in a recession and reap a hundred-fold return! It's good to know that there is no recession in God's Kingdom!

People, generally speaking, know that God is able. Even those who are not born again believe that God is able. We probably know people who know that God can heal. According to these people, whether God will heal or He won't is a different matter altogether. O, but brother Stan, you just never know what God will do! He can choose to heal or not heal. If He heals me, ok. If not, blessed be His Holy Name. Amen.

Give me a humongous break! Why not be astute enough and find out from His Word what He will or won't do? Take the topic we are studying at the moment for example. Will God heal you or not? We know He can, but will He?

Let's look at the following verse of Scripture.

> *And, behold, there came a leper and worshipped him, saying, Lord, if thou wilt, thou canst make me clean. And Jesus put forth his hand, and touched him, saying, I will; be thou clean. And immediately his leprosy was cleansed.* Matthew 8:2, 3

God *can* and God *will*! God *can* and God *will*!! I said, God *can* and God *will*! We need to let this phrase to repeatedly wash through our minds to get rid of any doubts in us as to whether He will or He won't. This kind of 'brain-wash' is healthy!

Look at this leper! He came to Jesus knowing very well that Jesus could heal him. He confession was, '*if thou wilt, thou canst'* and Jesus' responded with a *'I will'*. Since Jesus Christ is the same yesterday, today and forever, He *still* is willing to manifest, *today* and in your body, the healing *He* accomplished for you by the stripes that were laid on His back! If you need healing in your body, receive it right now in His Name!

It is important to establish where sicknesses and diseases come from. God has been blamed for a whole lot of mess that He never was involved in! God doesn't give out sicknesses and diseases. He has none to give out! The disciples of Jesus had this issue of 'who is giving what to who' all mixed up too! There is hope for all of us!

Look at the following Scripture.

> *And his disciples asked him, saying, Master, who did sin, this man, or his parents, that he was born blind? Jesus answered, Neither hath this man sinned, nor his parents: but that the works of God should be made manifest in him. I must work the works of him that sent me, while it is day: the night cometh, when no man can work. As long as I am in the world, I am the light of the world. When he had thus spoken, he spat on the ground, and made clay of the spittle, and he anointed the eyes of the blind man with the clay And said unto him, Go, wash in the pool of Siloam, (which is by interpretation, Sent.) He went his way therefore, and washed, and came seeing.*
> John 9:2-7

From the above account, we see Jesus setting the record straight as to the man's blind condition. Notice that Jesus responds by saying that neither the man nor his parents sinned for him to be born blind. He was a prime candidate for the works of God to be made manifest in Him! Now watch carefully what these works are. Jesus made clay with His spittle, anointed the eyes of the blind man, asked him to go and wash in the pool of Siloam and the man received his sight.

It is vital to note that Jesus had *nothing* to do with man being blind but *everything* to do with the man receiving his sight! I submit to you, therefore, that God had nothing to do with your sickness! Blame the devil for the sickness and thank God for your healing!

Now, there is an important question that I sense we need to answer right here. Is sickness a consequence of sin in one's life? Originally, I would say, yes. Adam and Eve sinned in the garden and invited the curse, and we know sickness is part of the curse. But do we get sick because of committing sin? In some cases, yes, and in others, no.

In the case of the blind man in the verse quoted above, Jesus categorically stated that sin had *nothing* to do with the man being born blind. But in some cases, sin *is* directly responsible for diseases.

Take for example, sexually transmitted diseases. These diseases are as a result of sexual promiscuity. The Bible calls it adultery or fornication, which *is* sin. Take lung cancer, for example. People smoke cigarettes, which, in turn, cause lung cancer. Even the cigarette manufacturers print labels to inform smokers that smoking is injurious to their health and yet people still smoke millions of 'sticks' daily! And then, the same people go and blame lung cancer on God! Come on!!! 'The Lord giveth, the Lord taketh away. Blessed be the Name of the Lord.' How daft can one get! It's like you taking a razor blade, slicing open your blood veins, bleed yourself to death and then blame it on God for bleeding to death! God had nothing to do with it! It was your blade and your hands that did the work!

So then, since we have seen that health is provided for us, let us enjoy this provision with thanks giving to God.

WEALTH

It is abundantly clear throughout the Bible, that God has provided wealth for those in covenant with Him. All the way back to Adam, God's provision for man to walk in wealth is evident. For God to turn the whole earth, and the fullness therefore, to *one* man and *one* woman called Adam and Even is a demonstration of His desire for man to live in abundant wealth! And what amount of wealth this was! Imagine what you could do if God turned over the entire earth, with all it's resources, over to you and your wife! Not even kids on drugs to mess up this scenario, either! Wao!

It is, and it has always been, God's plan for man to be so well provided for, to *actually* have surplus!

Let's first of all define the world 'wealth'.

> *But thou shalt remember the LORD thy God: for it is he that giveth thee power to get wealth, that he*

may establish his covenant which he sware unto thy fathers, as it is this day. Deuteronomy 8:18

The word, *'wealth'* in the above scripture, is translated from the Hebrew word, *'chayil'* (khah'-yil). It means, "a force, whether of men, means or other resources, an army, wealth activity, goods, host, might, power, riches, strength, strong substance, valiant, valor".

Notice here that it is God who gives us power to get wealth. His desire is that we become a force to reckon with, in material substance, riches, strength, armed forces, power, ability and valor! I'm sure there are no cowards reading this!

God put that word 'wealth' in the Bible and the definitions tell you exactly what He gives you the power to get! Wealth is ability! *'We can do all things through Christ that strengthens us'*! (Philippians 4:13)Wealth is riches! (Ephesians 1:18) Wealth is a force, whether of men, means or other resources!

For by thee I have run through a troop: by my God have I leaped over a wall. 2 Samuel 22:30

Wealth is valiant!

Through God we shall do valiantly: for he it is that shall tread down our enemies. Psalms 60:12

Expand your thinking and embrace the wealth God gives you the power to get!! Watch very closely the following verse.

And I will make thee exceeding fruitful, and I will make nations of thee, and kings shall come out of thee. Genesis 17:6

God's promise to Abraham is that God would make him exceeding fruitful! I find these two words 'exceeding, and fruitful' very interesting. Let's define them.

That word 'exceeding' is translated from the Hebrew word, *'me'od'* (meh'ode) which means, "vehemence or vehemently, wholly, speedily, diligently, especially, far, fast, good, great, might,(so)much, quickly, utterly, very, well."

The word 'fruitful' is translated from the Hebrew word, *'parah'* (paw-raw') which means, "to bear fruit, bring forth fruit, to be or cause to be fruitful, to make fruitful, grow, increase."

From these two definitions, we see that God was to "vehemently, wholly, speedily, fast, utterly, diligently, greatly and mighty" make Abraham to "bear fruit, grow and increase".

Observe carefully, also, that kings would come out of Abraham's loins! You and I know that kings are people of great means, wealthy beyond imagination! Why is it so important to know what God promised Abraham? Because the promises made to Abraham are ours also! God's covenant of blessing made to Abraham extends to us through Jesus Christ!

Notice what the scripture say in the following verse.

*Christ hath redeemed us from the curse of the law,
being made a curse for us: for it is written, Cursed is
every one that hangeth on a tree: That the blessing
of Abraham might come on the Gentiles through
Jesus Christ; that we might receive the promise of
the Spirit through faith.* Galatians 3:13, 14

Since Christ has redeemed us from the curse of the law so
that the blessing of Abraham may be ours, shouldn't we
lay claim on what *rightfully* belongs to us?

Going by the earlier definitions, God wants to make us
exceedingly fruitful! And fast!! We will be looking at laws
that govern increase later on in the book, but notice here
that God is Diligent and vehement about increasing us! He
does not want us to barely have enough but rather to be
utterly wealth!

Now, go back to the definitions of 'exceeding' and 'fruitful'
and read the Scripture verse with those definitions in mind
and it will bless 'your socks off' It might be new to you,
but it is God!

And if you thought that was too much, wait till you read
the following verse!

*And it shall come to pass, if thou shalt hearken
diligently unto the voice of the LORD thy God, to
observe and to do all his commandments which I
command thee this day, that the LORD thy God will
set thee on high above all nations of the earth: And*

all these blessings shall come on thee, and over-take thee, if thou shalt hearken unto the voice of the LORD thy God. Blessed shalt thou be in the city, and blessed shalt thou be in the field. Deuteronomy 28:1-3

*And it shall come to pass,…*What a comforting thing to know that God's Word is a sure thing! There is no guessing, hit or miss gamble when it comes to the Promises of God! It shall come to pass… When will it come to pass? The above-quoted scripture indicates that God's desire for it *'to come to pass' is now*. We saw earlier that God is diligent in making us fruitful. The 'when', therefore, is dependent on our obedience to His Word! The sooner we obey His Word 'it will come to pass'!

Watch closely here when He says that blessings shall come upon us and overtake us. The word 'blessings' is trans-lated from the Hebrew word, *'Berahak'* (ber-aw-kaw'). Two renditions of the word 'blessing' that I really like are 'prosperity' and 'liberal'. God will liberally prosper those who are diligent to observe and do His Word, to the point that blessings *will* come upon them and overtake them! We are establishing that wealth is God's will for you and me!

Notice what the following verse of Scripture has to say.

The LORD shall open unto thee his good treasure, the heaven to give the rain unto thy land in his season, and to bless all the work of thine hand: and thou shalt lend unto many nations, and thou shalt not borrow. Deuteronomy 28:12

Somebody's view of God is going to be radically changed by this verse! Some people have always viewed God as a close-fisted, stingy miser who hardly ever releases a penny to bless His children! Nothing could be farther from the truth!!

In the first place, notice that God has a good treasure! Not a junk-yard, but a good treasure!

Now, I don't know whether your imagination is as active as mine, but, the word 'treasure' brings to my mind captain hook going on a treasure hunt on Treasure Island. I imagine all those jewels, necklaces, golden bric-a-bracs and precious stones overflowing the treasure chests on Treasure Island. Oh hallelujah! And now God stimulates my imagination when He says that He opens His good treasure to His covenant man! I'm calling Him for my share of the treasure! I'm going for mine and you better go for you yours, too! There is enough treasure for everybody!

That word 'treasure' is translated from the Hebrew word, *'owtsar'* (o-tsaw') which means, "a depository, armory, cellar, garner, store-house, treasure-house".

Evidently, God has a 'depository', which He opens and gives access to His covenant man! This 'depository' would be what we ordinarily call a bank. When God opens and pours out to us His good treasure, we become so wealthy that we have no need to borrow or take a loan from the local bank! In actual fact, the opposite holds true! We are the ones lending, not only to banks, but to nations!!

Now, now, brother Stan, you are taking this a bit too far! I think not. I don't think I'm taking it far enough! God is bigger than our wildest imaginations, infinitely superior to what our finite minds can fathom or comprehend! What I'm doing is just writing what is written in the Bible! And if I can see it in the word, then I can have it! And so can you, too!!

> *And God is able to make all grace abound toward you; that ye, always having all sufficiency in all things, may abound to every good work:* 2 Corinthians 9:8

We said earlier in the book that God *can* and God *will* do what He said He will do. The above verse shows us that it is God's will for us to have all sufficiency in all things to the extent we are giving unto *every* good work! You can't give that which you don't have. You can't do 'good' if you have nothing to do 'good' with. That is why God desires for us to be so well supplied with His blessings that we are able to extend His goodness to others!

Chapter five

Wealth by the word

"Godly wealth is a
Product of the Word,
And not of the world"
Wangenye

———❦———

W e need to understand that Godly wealth is produced by the Word of God and not by any geographical location! A covenant man is prosperous, no matter where he or she may have born. Whatever part of town or village you may be from is inconsequential in the eyes of God. Whether the flag of your country has bars, stripes, rectangle, squares, red, blue, white or whatever other color, really holds no water in the eyes of God! None of all that is a determinant factor in your acquiring wealth. Godly wealth is a product of the Word of God.

Oh, but brother Stan, I'm from Africa. So? Is God not in Africa? I guarantee you, He is! Oh, but, I'm from a third world country with inadequate resources for me to get wealthy.

In the first place, *did* God classify countries as first, second and third world or is it someone else's daft idea? Are we not *all* born equal in the eyes of God or are some more 'equal' than others? Every nation in the eyes of God is as important as the next! It is the choices nations make that determine whether they are blessed or reproached! The Bible states very clearly that:

> *Righteousness exalteth a nation: but sin is a reproach to any people.* Proverbs 14:34

My considered opinion is that all that 'third world' classification is just high class nonsense and should be gotten out of your thinking! Think on what God says about you, not some economist!

And who said you are without resources? Who said developing economies are without resources? Look at Africa! A continent that is so endowed with human, mineral and natural resources, its mind-boggling! Look around you and see all the God-given possibilities that people in Africa have to become wealthy! Stop whining and complaining and dig in from the resources of the Word of God!! With His Word, you *will* get such witty ideas that you may be selling sea water by the sea-shore and sand in the desert the next time I see you! And people may be fighting one another just to be able to do business with you!

Look at the following Scripture again.

> *But thou shalt remember the LORD thy God: for it is he that giveth thee power to get wealth, that he may establish his covenant which he sware unto thy fathers, as it is this day.* Deuteronomy 8:18

It is God that gives us *power* to get *wealth*! No matter the location you may find yourself in, this *power* is available for you to get *wealth*. That word 'power' is translated from the Hebrew word, '*koach*' (ko'-ach) which means, "to be firm, vigor, force, capacity, means to produce, ability, might."

God, in essence, is telling us that it is He that gives us the capacity, means to produce and the ability to get wealth. Let's look at another Scripture.

> *This book of the law shall not depart out of thy mouth; but thou shalt meditate therein day and night, that thou mayest observe to do according to*

all that is written therein: for then thou shalt make thy way prosperous, and then thou shalt have good success. Joshua 1: 8

Joshua, in taking over leadership of God's people after the death of Moses, got his formula for prosperity straight from God Himself!

'This book of the law....' *is* talking about the Word of God. Prosperity for you and me *will* be produced when we *'observe to do all that is written therein'*. God's Word hasn't changed, nor will it ever change. He is no respecter of persons or places! In fact, He seems to, at times; prosper the most unlikely people in the most unlikely locations on planet earth just to prove that, *all* that is required is the application of His Word! It must give God a thrill to graduate His children from 'zeros to heroes', 'down and outs' to 'up and about'. And *you* are not a case too difficult for God to bless! Hallelujah!!

Look at that scripture again.

And it shall come to pass, if thou shalt hearken diligently unto the voice of the LORD thy God, to observe and to do all his commandments which I command thee this day, that the LORD thy God will set thee on high above all nations of the earth: And all these blessings shall come on thee, and overtake thee, if thou shalt hearken unto the voice of the LORD thy God. Blessed shalt thou be in the city, and blessed shalt thou be in the field. Deuteronomy 28: 1-3

Notice that God's blessings are non-territorial! Ours is to hearken diligently unto the voice of the Lord our God, to observe and to do all His word, and blessings will come upon us and overtake us! In the city or in the field, in the UK, in Kenya, Timbuktu, USA or which ever country you may be living in.

God's blessing will find you out!! God knows your address and will find you out to bless you! Praise the Lord!

SECTION 2

GODLY
WEALTH

Chapter six

Foundations
For Godly wealth

"Get it God's way.
No other way is worth it!"
Wangenye

———∞∞∞———

Every building that is going to weather the storms of life must be founded on a firm foundation. How important is a foundation?

Look at what Christ had to say about it.

> *Therefore whosoever heareth these sayings of mine, and doeth them, I will liken him unto a wise man, which built his house upon a rock: And the rain descended, and the floods came, and the winds blew, and beat upon that house; and it fell not: for it was founded upon a rock. And every one that heareth these sayings of mine, and doeth them not, shall be likened unto a foolish man, which built his house upon the sand: And the rain descended, and the floods came, and the winds blew, and beat upon that house; and it fell: and great was the fall of it.*
> Matthew 7: 24-27

Notice here that Jesus is warning us about impending storms of life. He is not saying any one of us is exempt from storms. What determines whether a house will withstand a storm or not is the foundation on which it is built on. The foundation will also determine how high the building can be built. Sky-scrappers need a very deep, firm foundation to support all that weight. And so do our lives. Without proper foundations, people's lives are prone to be pulled down by winds and storms of life!

Notice Jesus, in the above Scripture, says, that hearing and not doing His Word *is* like building without a proper foundation. When the storm hits, that house is coming down. On the other hand, hearing and doing what God says to us *is* likened to building on a firm foundation. Though the storms of life *will* come, *nothing* will bring you down, once you find the Rock and build your life on Him by hearing and doing what He says! Hallelujah!!

In earlier chapters, we established that its God will for us to prosper. In this chapter, we are going to lay a firm foundation, based on God's Word, on our claim to Godly wealth, which is brought about by our observing to do all that is written in God's Word.

Our first area of obedience to God's Word is:

FIRSTFRUITS

The genesis of our claim to Godly wealth is our obeying God in the principle of offering the first-fruits. Now, what in the world is that?

It is a little-understood principle straight from your Bible, and this principle is about to bless your socks off, so hang on!

And in process of time it came to pass, that Cain brought of the fruit of the ground an offering unto the LORD. And Abel, he also brought of the firstlings of his flock and of the fat thereof. And the LORD had respect unto Abel and to his offering: But unto Cain and to his offering he had not respect. And Cain was very wroth, and his countenance fell. And the LORD said unto Cain, Why art thou wroth? and why is thy countenance fallen? If thou doest well, shalt thou not be accepted? and if thou doest not well, sin lieth at the door. And unto thee shall be his desire, and thou shalt rule over him. Genesis 4: 3-7

We begin at the first record in the Bible of man coming to worship and sacrifice to God. Before we see the significance of the *kind* of sacrifices offered by Cain and Abel, let me first of all bring to our attention the fact that, every man born into this world has an in-built, automatic desire to worship something. A side thought here: we can't possibly worship without sacrificing! Anyway, that's another book, altogether!

But to stay with what we are talking about here, man's natural response to being born into this world is a desire to worship. *(Apart from the desire to eat and mess up, that is.)* It is instructive to note that many, even in the Church, have forsaken the worship of Jehovah Elohiym, the Creator, and have turned to the worship of created things! Wealth, power, fame, careers, status, flashy automobiles, designer wear and just about everything else that is fashionable, have captured the worship of many a man, thereby filling man with the spirit of the world! The 'thing' which man worships, the spirit of the object thereof fills him up! If you worship Jehovah, His Spirit will fill you up! If you worship worldly things, the spirit of the world will fill you up! The choice is yours! Wisdom would have you to turn your eyes upon Jesus, look full into His wonderful face and things of earth will grow dim, enabling you to worship Jehovah!

As far as I could tell, there is no record in the Bible where we see Adam instructing Cain and Abel of the need to worship God. Yet we see them coming to worship God and bringing their sacrifices. He may have, but we are not told.

I have heard it preached that God had no respect for Cain or his sacrifice because his sacrifice wasn't a blood sacrifice. While that may be so, I do believe that the *main* reason why God had no respect for Cain or his sacrifice was because Cain *did not* observe the firstling, first-fruit, first-born principle! Sacrifice is acceptable to God, whether of fruits or of animal.

Notice what the scriptures say:

> *And all the tithe of the land, whether of the seed of the land, or of the fruit of the tree, is the LORD'S: it is holy unto the LORD. And if a man will at all redeem ought of his tithes, he shall add thereto the fifth part thereof. And concerning the tithe of the herd, or of the flock, even of whatsoever passeth under the rod, the tenth shall be holy unto the LORD.* Leviticus 27:30-32

> *Thou mayest not eat within thy gates the tithe of thy corn, or of thy wine, or of thy oil, or the firstlings of thy herds or of thy flock, nor any of thy vows which thou vowest, nor thy freewill offerings, or heave offering of thine hand:* Deuteronomy 12:17

We note in the above Scriptures, God categorically stating that *all* the tithe, whether it's the fruit of the tree or the herd of the cattle, is His!

Since this fact is so vividly clear from the above scriptures, God's rejection of Cain and his sacrifice, then, may not have been due to the fact that he brought fruits! What Cain did not do was to bring the *first-fruit*! Abel brought the *firstling* and honored God in the thing that opened the matrix. Cain did not! He thought *just* an offering would do, but it didn't and it still doesn't!

Do you mean to say that there is a difference between the tithe and first-fruits? Most certainly! The firstborn of every family, of every cattle, the first-fruit of every new farm, the increment of every pay-raise, the first salary of every new job, every single penny thereof belong to God! I mean, when you get employed, the *entire* first pay-check belongs to God!

But how will you live in the meantime, you might ask. Well, how *were* you living *before* God gave you the job? Why has it now become so difficult to honor God now that He has given you a job? Watch what God says in the following Scripture.

That thou shalt set apart unto the LORD all that openeth the matrix, and every firstling that cometh of a beast which thou hast; the males shall be the LORD'S. And every firstling of an ass thou shalt redeem with a lamb; and if thou wilt not redeem it, then thou shalt break his neck: and all the firstborn of man among thy children shalt thou redeem. And it shall be when thy son asketh thee in time to come, saying, What is this? that thou shalt say unto him, By strength of hand the LORD brought us out from Egypt, from the house of bondage: And it came to pass, when Pharaoh would hardly let us go, that the LORD slew all the firstborn in the land of Egypt, both the firstborn of man, and the firstborn of beast: therefore I sacrifice to the LORD all that openeth the matrix, being males; but all the firstborn of my children I redeem. Exodus 13:12-15

All that openeth the matrix is mine; and every first-ling among thy cattle, whether ox or sheep, that is male. But the firstling of an ass thou shalt redeem with a lamb: and if thou redeem him not, then shalt thou break his neck. All the firstborn of thy sons thou shalt redeem. And none shall appear before me empty. Exodus 34:19-20

All that open the matrix or the womb belong to God! *All* means *all*! When you get that pay raise, *all* of that increase belongs to God *plus* the tithe *and* offerings of whatever you used to earn!

Notice how serious God took (and still does) the firstling principle.

Verse 13 of Exodus 13 instructed the people of God to redeem the firstling of an ass with a lamb. If you didn't redeem the ass, you were to break its neck! If you didn't break his neck, the very water he drew for you would be cursed, the goods he carried for you would be cursed! In other words, if you didn't redeem the firstling of the ass, break its neck because it would bring in a curse into your family!

If you didn't give the first-fruits, first check or the first profit from your business, you might as well throw them out with the garbage because failure to do so invites the curse! Ouch! Ouch! You just heard the truth!

It is instructive to note that God is not into human sacrifice! Every firstborn son had to be redeemed! There was no question of breaking his neck, like you did to the ass! Human life is so sacred to God that He redeemed it with the Lamb of God, Jesus Christ! Praise the Lord!

We are to offer our first-fruits to God *in acknowledgement* of our redemption *and* His provision. It is a memorial of what God has done in saving us and bringing us into a land that flows with milk and honey, of gratitude towards God in all He has done for us and in us.

You may not have known this in times past, but now you do.

> *And the times of this ignorance God winked at; but now commandeth all men every where to repent:* Acts 17:30

Let me make something absolutely clear. First-fruits are given once for any given business, employment or pay raise. For example, if the Lord blesses you with a job paying £2000 a week, only the first week is deemed first-fruit! For all subsequent weeks, you only pay tithes and offering, that is £200 plus whatever free will offering you wish to give. When the Lord grants you a pay raise to £2400 a week, the *first* raise of £400 plus the tithe of £240 *plus* free will offerings belong to God! The raise is payable once! In the following weeks after your pay the first-fruits raise, you will only be required to pay a tithe of £240 plus free will offering. I trust this is clear to all of us.

TITHES AND OFFERINGS

We earlier read how God repeatedly say to us that we are to diligently observe to do all that is written in His Word, the Bible.

So let us see what He has to say about the tithe.

> *And he saith unto them, Whose is this image and superscription They say unto him, Caesar's. Then saith he unto them, Render therefore unto Caesar the things which are Caesar's; and unto God the things that are God's.* Matthew 22:20-21

In my Bible, the above words are in red, signifying that Jesus *actually* spoke them out of His own mouth. He was, at this point, being tempted by the Pharisees as to whether it was lawful to pay taxes or not. What I want you to really observe is His reply to the temptation! He doesn't dispute with them but goes straight to the heart of the matter, *'Give to Caesar the things that belong to Caesar, and to God the things that belong to God'*.

Since we are commanded by Jesus Himself to give to God the things that belong to God, the wisest thing to do is to obey Him! By Jesus so emphatically stating that we should give to God the *things* that belong to God, it must mean that *there are* things in our possession, right now, that don't belong to us, but to God! Why else would Jesus *command* us to give *to God* those things that belong to God, if we didn't have things that belong to Him?

Let us identify what those things are.

The tithe *is* the lord's! To some, this may come as a revelation while to others, it will be a reminder. The tithe *truly* is the Lord's. It is holy unto the Lord! Render unto Caesar the things that are Caesar's and unto God the things that belong to God.

It is an indictment against the body of Christ that they have been faithful to render unto Caesar the things that are Caesar's, and, largely, ignored God financially altogether! If you don't think so, how many times have you missed paying your taxes? How often do you miss paying the electricity or phone bill, without the utility company disconnecting you? On the other hand, how many times do you miss paying God His tithe? Ouch! You might not want to answer that one! This word is not meant to condemn you but I pray that you get thoroughly convicted, repent and start paying the tithe!

How much of the tithe are we to pay to the Lord? We just read it. *All* the tithe! Gross or net? Read the following Scripture for your answer!

Thou shalt truly tithe all the increase of thy seed, that the field bringeth forth year by year. And thou shalt eat before the LORD thy God, in the place which he shall choose to place his name there, the tithe of thy corn, of thy wine, and of thine oil, and the firstlings of thy herds and of thy flocks; that thou mayest learn to fear the LORD thy God always. And if the way be too long for thee, so that thou art not able to carry it; or if the place be too far from thee, which the LORD thy God shall choose to set his name there, when the LORD thy God hath blessed thee: Then shalt thou turn it into money, and bind up the money in thine hand, and shalt go unto the place which the LORD thy God shall choose: Deuteronomy 14:22-25

*Thou shalt truly tithe all the increase of thy seed...*Why would God have to include the word, *'truly'*, in the above Scripture? Why would He go to the trouble of saying *'you shall truly tithe all'*? Couldn't He have simply said *'you shall tithe'* and that would have sufficed? No Sir!! God knows good and well that His people are liable to cheat! Don't shout me down, now! I'm preaching *real* good! He knows this is a generation that is eager to *'net'* their seeds and *'gross'* their harvest! A people inclined to sow the least possible seed and harvest the largest possible harvest! Listen! There are no short cuts in the Kingdom of God! Nor can you con God! You reap *exactly* what you sow! If you *'net'* your giving, *'net'* harvest and blessings are heading your way!

And God didn't complicate the arithmetic, either! He gave us the percentage that is easiest to calculate! 10%! Now, no matter how much you hated math, you *at least* can calculate the tenth part of your pay! If you unable to calculate the 10%, try your fingers and thumbs, since there are ten of them! In case you run out, remove your shoes and stocks and continue on your toes. You have ten of those, too, you know! In case the above fails, call for the elders of the church to pray for you with the laying on of hands!

Per adventure thou 'mayest' see the 'arithmetic' light! The whole point is, *truly* tithe and no cheating!

It may be that some will try to wriggle out of this by saying they are farmers without a salary. God got their number, too! When you sell the produce of your land, bring 10% tithe of the profit from the sales to Church! That is what the above Scripture says! And while you are at it, *truly* tithe and no cheating!

How do we know it is 10% and not 12%?

Let us read what the Bible says about this.

> *And Melchizedek king of Salem brought forth bread and wine: and he was the priest of the most high God. And he blessed him, and said, Blessed be Abram of the most high God, possessor of heaven and earth: And blessed be the most high God, which hath delivered thine enemies into thy hand. And he gave him tithes of all.* Genesis 14:18-20

> *And this stone, which I have set for a pillar, shall be God's house: and of all that thou shalt give me I will surely give the tenth unto thee.* Genesis 28:22

The Hebrew word for 'tithe' as recorded in Genesis 14: 20, is; *'ma'aser'*, (mah-as-ayr') It translates to; "a tenth; tenth (part)". Genesis 28:22 makes it absolutely clear as to what Jacob was vowing to give to God: a tenth part of all God blessed him with.

Now, on to one of the most famous portion of the Scriptures related to tithe.

> *Bring ye all the tithes into the storehouse, that there may be meat in mine house, and prove me now herewith, saith the LORD of hosts, if I will not open you the windows of heaven, and pour you out a blessing, that there shall not be room enough to receive it.* Malachi 3:10

I think the only reason why *anyone* would wish this verse was not in the Bible was because they don't understand its purpose!

God is not out to take from you, but He is out to bless you! He is looking for every available opportunity to bless you! He has declared that, when you and I tithe, He *will* open the windows of heaven and pour out a blessing to the extent that we won't have room enough to receive it! Now, that is increase! God's principle of receiving is realized when we give. So, obey the Lord in this joyfully, knowing that God is setting you up for a blessing! Amen!

Is the tithe only in the Old Testament? No sir! We are the New Testament church obeying both the Old and the New Testaments!

Turn to Hebrews, if you will please.

> *And here men that die receive tithes; but there he receiveth them, of whom it is witnessed that he liveth.* Hebrews 7:8

'Here men that die receive tithes.' This must mean that you are to pay tithe here on earth so that *'men that die'* receive them! These *'men that die'* are anyone of the five fold ministry officers that *consistently* feed you with the Word of God and have spiritual oversight over you! I realize this might not go down very well with some Pastors, but you just heard the truth!

Let us look at the book of Matthew.

> *Woe unto you, scribes and Pharisees, hypocrites! for ye pay tithe of mint and anise and cummin, and have omitted the weightier matters of the law, judgment, mercy, and faith: these ought ye to have done, and not to leave the other undone.* Matthew 23:23

Again, in my Bible, the above words are in red, signifying that Jesus Christ *actually* spoke them out of His own mouth. Watch carefully what He says.

Jesus rebuked the Pharisees for doing something and leaving the other undone. Notice Jesus *did not* rebuke them for paying their tithe, but rather for leaving weightier matters of the law, judgment, mercy and faith undone. In other words, He told them that they should have paid their tithes *as well as* observe the weightier matters of the law, judgment, mercy and faith!

WHY DO WE TITHE?

1.   Because it is a command.

This day the LORD thy God hath commanded thee to do these statutes and judgments: thou shalt therefore keep and do them with all thine heart, and with all thy soul. Deuteronomy26:16

You may not have known that paying your tithe is a commandment from God, but today, you just read the above Scripture! *'This day the Lord thy God has commanded you to do this statutes and judgments'.*

If you read verses 1 to 25 of the same chapter, you will see the commandment God is giving you regards paying the tithes and offerings that are holy unto the Lord. Obedience to the Lord in paying the tithe is our duty as children of our heavenly Father. The tithe is His and it is a debt we owe Him. The command from Him is to pay up His tithe and then sow offerings as seeds of faith!

2. Because we love God.

If ye love me, keep my commandments. John 14:15

Honour the LORD with thy substance, and with the firstfruits of all thine increase: Proverbs 3:9

If we claim to love God, then we will keep His commandment! In fact, one of the best ways to show that we love God and honor Him is through giving! God Himself so loved the world that He gave His only begotten Son. His demonstration of love, His prove of His love, was made manifest through His giving us His Son, Jesus Christ. Had He not given, His love would have been in question, but since He gave, His love *is* guaranteed! Confirm, affirm and demonstrate your love for God through paying Him His tithe!

3.   To activate the law of increase.

Bring ye all the tithes into the storehouse, that there may be meat in mine house, and prove me now herewith, saith the LORD of hosts, if I will not open you the windows of heaven, and pour you out a blessing, that there shall not be room enough to receive it. Malachi 3:10

Give, and it shall be given unto you; good measure, pressed down, and shaken together, and running over, shall men give into your bosom. For with the same measure that ye mete withal it shall be measured to you again. Luke 6:38

Notice that this is also a reason for paying God's tithes and giving our offerings! When we obey God in bringing His tithes to the storehouse, we activate increase as He responds by opening the windows of heaven and pouring us a blessing, to the extent of us not having room enough to contain it all! Now, that is what I call increase! We will discuss this law in detail in the next chapter.

HOW SHOULD WE GIVE?

*   By faith

But without faith it is impossible to please him: for he that cometh to God must believe that he is, and that he is a rewarder of them that diligently seek him. Hebrews 11:6

Everything in the kingdom of God works by faith! Without faith, it doesn't matter how religious one is. The bottom line is, without faith, it is impossible to please God!

When we give by faith, we put God on top of the expenditure list. He should not be the last one to get what is coming to Him, but, rather, He should be the first! We tithe and give offerings *first, believing* God that the remaining 80-85% of our income will be sufficient to meet our needs! We do not hold back our giving to see how things will turn out later on the month! No sir!! We give it when we have it at hand!

Withhold not good from them to whom it is due, when it is in the power of thine hand to do it. Say not unto thy neighbour, Go, and come again, and to morrow I will give; when thou hast it by thee. Proverbs 3:27-28

• Joyfully

The spirit in which we give is an expression of the condition of our heart. A heart of gratitude will always give God joyfully, not begrudging what he is giving! And our heavenly Father rejoices over a cheerful giver!

Every man according as he purposeth in his heart, so let him give; not grudgingly, or of necessity: for God loveth a cheerful giver. 2 Corinthians 9:7

This is good, but let's looks at the same Scripture from the Amplified version of the Bible.

> *Let each one (give) as he has made up his own mind and purposed in his heart, not reluctantly or sorrowfully or under compulsion, for God loves (He takes pleasure in, prizes above other things, and is unwilling to abandon or to do without) a cheerful (joyous, "prompt to do it") giver (whose heart is in his giving).* 2 Corinthians 9:7 (Amplified)

The Amplified is a mouthful but it really opens up to us the heart of God where giving joyfully is concerned!

- Liberally

We know that nobody really likes or wants to be around a stingy, close-fisted miser! Well. Neither does God!

> *There is that scattereth, and yet increaseth; and there is that withholdeth more than is meet, but it tendeth to poverty. The liberal soul shall be made fat: and he that watereth shall be watered also himself.* Proverbs 11:24-25

God delights in a liberal soul so much, that, He fattens him up! Now, before you dieting, weight-watching generation revolt against the word, 'fat', listen to what it means! It is translated from the Hebrew word; 'dashen' means, to satisfy. A liberal soul shall be anointed and satisfied! Glory to God!

WHAT SHOULD WE GIVE?

The best! We give God *our* best as we expect *His* best! If we are to honor God in our giving, then it is imperative that we give the best we can! In fact, He not only deserves the best, but He also expects it!

> *A son honoureth his father, and a servant his master: if then I be a father, where is mine honour? and if I be a master, where is my fear? saith the LORD of hosts unto you, O priests, that despise my name. And ye say, Wherein have we despised thy name? Ye offer polluted bread upon mine altar; and ye say, Wherein have we polluted thee? In that ye say, The table of the LORD is contemptible. And if ye offer the blind for sacrifice, is it not evil? and if ye offer the lame and sick, is it not evil? offer it now unto thy governor; will he be pleased with thee, or accept thy person? saith the LORD of hosts.* Malachi 1:6-8

Please note in the above Scripture, that, to offer a lame or blind sacrifice is evil in the eyes of God! It does not honor God when we offer gifts that we wouldn't even *dream* of offering to earthly dignitaries! Why is the quality of your gift so important? This is because your gift or offering signifies the value or esteem that you ascribe to the one you are giving the gift to. That is why God challenges those priests in Malachi to try and offer the kind of offerings they were offering to Him, to their governor! It would not come as a surprise if they were denied audience with the governor on account of their offering!

Watch closely the following Scripture.

> *And in process of time it came to pass, that Cain brought of the fruit of the ground an offering unto the LORD. And Abel, he also brought of the firstlings of his flock and of the fat thereof. And the LORD had respect unto Abel and to his offering: But unto Cain and to his offering he had not respect. And Cain was very wroth, and his countenance fell. And the LORD said unto Cain, Why art thou wroth? and why is thy countenance fallen? If thou doest well, shalt thou not be accepted? and if thou doest not well, sin lieth at the door. And unto thee shall be his desire, and thou shalt rule over him.* Genesis 4:3-7

We had looked at this Scripture while discussing the principle of the first-fruits, but there is so much in this Scripture that it bears repeating!

Please note here that Cain and Abel came to worship the Lord *with* material substance! God respected Abel and his sacrifice but did not do the same for Cain. Knowing that God is no respecter of persons, the reason as to why God had respect for Abel and not for Cain must, therefore, be in the sacrifices they brought.

Notice that Cain brought *just an offering* of the fruit of the ground but Abel brought of the *firstlings* of his flock and of the fat thereof! Abel did not just bring the firstlings, he brought the fat also! He demonstrates that he was not just trying to get by, by giving the *least* amount possible! He added 'fat' to his firstlings! Now, what did Cain do? He nonchalantly brought an offering and that was it! Like we said earlier, I don't believe that the fact that Cain brought the fruit of the ground automatically disqualified him from being acceptable to God. Remember *Leviticus 27:30*? It states:

> *And all the tithe of the land, whether of the seed of the land, or of the fruit of the tree, is the LORD'S: it is holy unto the LORD.*

I believe that the fact that Cain did not give the first-fruits nor did he give *his* best disqualified him from being accepted! God actually told him that if he did well, he would be accepted!

Let us not try to get by with the *least* amount possible, but let us approach God with the best offering possible.

WHERE DO WE GIVE?

On good ground! Any smart farmer sows his seed on good ground! This is because it is *only* good that guarantees a harvest.

> *Hearken; Behold, there went out a sower to sow: And it came to pass, as he sowed, some fell by the way side, and the fowls of the air came and devoured it up. And some fell on stony ground, where it had not much earth; and immediately it sprang up, because it had no depth of earth: But when the sun was up, it was scorched; and because it had no root, it withered away. And some fell among thorns, and the thorns grew up, and choked it, and it yielded no fruit. And other fell on good ground, and did yield fruit that*

sprang up and increased; and brought forth, some thirty, and some sixty, and some an hundred. Mark 4:3-8

Only *one* type of ground in the parable quoted above yielded a harvest! It is vital for us to understand that we are responsible for where we sow our seed. There is absolutely no time left for us to waste good seed on bad ground! Not that it was ever a good idea to throw seed away in the first place! But now, more than ever, we need to sow our seed in productive ground for the timely global harvest of souls to take place.

Notice also that this is *the only* ground where you personally *will* receive a harvest! In the above quoted Scripture, the Amplified version of the Bible states that it is the same kind of seed that was being sown on the different kinds of ground.

There is God-given ability and capacity for seeds to produce a harvest! In fact, there is awesome, miracle-working power in the seed that is in your hand right now! Whether that power is released to produce the maximum miracle possible or not, is dependent on whether you sow the seed and on the type of ground you sow into! Wisdom would have it that you sow your seed on the best ground possible within your reach so that you may receive your miracle harvest, in Jesus Name! Amen.

Chapter Seven

The law that governs increase

———∞∞∞———

Since we have established that it is God's will for us to be prosperous, how do we enter into that prosperity? In this section, we will study the law that governs increase.

While the laws outlined in the following chapter are applicable to the whole prosperity message, I would like us to specifically study wealth or monetary increase. God definitely desires that we be rich in monetary terms.

Let us study some Scriptures as we put forth a case for monetary increase as the Will of God for your life.

> *The blessing of the LORD, it maketh rich, and he addeth no sorrow with it.* Proverbs 10:22

> *Let them shout for joy, and be glad, that favour my righteous cause: yea, let them say continually, Let the LORD be magnified, which hath pleasure in the prosperity of his servant.* Psalms 35:27

God *actually* takes pleasure in the prosperity of His servants! I can just imagine God up in heaven taking pleasure *because* I prospered! I mean, He develops that good taste in His mouth just because His servant is doing well financially! He just feels good and that feel-good factor is being brought on by the prosperity of His servants! O Glory!

Watch this, now! His blessing makes us rich, not poor! The daft doctrine that poverty is godly directly contradicts the Scripture we just read!! When He says His blessing makes us rich, what part of 'rich' don't people understand?!! Hey!! Why would He bless us with something He doesn't want us to have? The argument that God wants us poor *just* doesn't add up! God definitely wants us blessed and *that* blessing will make us rich!

The Cardinal law or Principle that governs the increase of wealth can be stated in one verse of Scripture.

> *Give, and it shall be given unto you; good measure, pressed down, and shaken together, and running over, shall men give into your bosom. For with the same measure that ye mete withal it shall be measured to you again.* Luke 6:38

The 'law of increase' states: *"with the same measure that ye mete withal it shall be measured to you again"*.

Let's define some words here so that we can better understand what we just heard!

That word, *'measure'* is translated from the Greek word *'metron'* (met'-ron). In English, it means "a measure, as in "metre", a limited portion or degree". The measure or 'metre' we use governs and determines our harvest or our returns!

Notice I have not limited this definition to the giving done in tithes and offerings! This cardinal law of increase covers the giving you do in the entirety of your existence! If you give little effort in your work place, do no be shocked when your boss gives you a 'little' pay-check! If you give your skills using a big measure to the firm employing you, it is only right that you receive a pay-check commensurate of your input! A farmer desirous of a larger harvest must enlarge the measure he uses to sow his seed!

Now, if you are like me, you don't usually use the word "mete" in you every day speech. So, let's find out what that word means.

It is translated from the Greek word, *'metreo'* (met-reh'-o) which means, "to measure, ascertain in size by a fixed standard, allot by rule".

The major point we learn from the above definition is that, *you* are the one who ascertain the size of your harvest! If you use a small measure, you are guaranteed a small harvest, at the very best! No matter how much you pray, there is a rule or fixed standard that govern your harvest!

Your harvest does not respond to prayer, first of all, but rather, to the application of the seed principle! You can pray until the cows come home, but you'll still have no harvest because harvest only answers to the law of seed! Now, the size of the harvest directly responds to the 'mete' used in sowing!

Let us take this a step further. Look with me at another Scripture.

But this I say, He which soweth sparingly shall reap also sparingly; and he which soweth bountifully shall reap also bountifully. 2 Corinthians 9:6

Notice here that if one sows sparingly, he also shall reap sparingly! If one is desirous of a large increase, he must sow a large seed! Why is this so? Because .....

The law of increase is a reciprocal law

Reciprocal simply means that it waits for you to initiate the process and then it acts in turn. The size of the seed you sow will directly determine the size of the harvest you reap.

Just as it is in the natural, you cannot possibly reap a harvest of potatoes except you sow potato seeds! And if you only sow *one* potato, you possibly cannot expect to harvest 10,000 tones of potatoes! That *just* does not happen!! And the same holds true in every realm of our existence, *including* the spirit realm.

The law of increase presupposes that everyone has something that will be increase by the application of the law. This is true and we will be quoting from the Scriptures in just a moment.

But before we do so, I would like to first define the word 'law' for you. One of the definitions of '*law*', as defined in the English dictionary is, "a rule of action established by authority". This is really good! We need to understand that God operates through laws. He has established some rules of action for us to operate by, so as to get predictable results. Even our very salvation operates on the *law* of the Spirit of life in Christ Jesus making us free from the *law* of sin and death! (Romans 8:2) O Glory!!

Watch this! Key statement coming up! *The application of law brings predictable results!* Whenever and wherever a law is applied, you can predict the result with 100% accuracy! Why? Because the application of law brings predictable results! Take an apple, throw it in the air. Can you predict what *will* happen to that apple in about 3 seconds? I believe you can! You are an A+ student! Now, why did the apple behave the way *you* predicted? Because you applied a law which brings predictable results! And the same holds true in the realm of the spirit!

Nothing in God happens accidentally, coincidentally, magically or automatically! Everything waits for a law to be activated or acted upon, which in turn initiates or provokes, a resultant reaction! It reciprocates the law you activated! It responds to your action of application of the law of increase! Are you getting this?

Take creation, for example. All the ingredients were in place, the Spirit moving upon the face of the deep, the Word was with God in Heaven, yet *nothing* was happening until God said: *"let there be light"*, And light was! Just popped *right* out of darkness *in response* to an activation of law! (Genesis 1: 1-3) What law did God activate? The law of faith! (Romans 3:27) How did the law of faith get activated? By speaking!

Watch this!

> *But what saith it? The word is nigh thee, even in thy mouth, and in thy heart: that is, the word of faith, which we preach;* Romans 10:8

God *had to* speak out to activate the law of faith! He called things that *'be not'* as though they were and they became or appeared! (Romans 4:17) Whatsoever *'things'* that were in God's Heart had to be spoken out verbally for the law of faith to *'kick in'* and manifest the said things! Wao!

This would suggest to us that light was in darkness all along *waiting* to reciprocate the activation of a law which had a predictable result! There was *no way* light could not 'be' *because* it was governed by law (a rule of action established by authority)! It *had* to respond to law! Hallelujah!

Another example. Let's go back to that potato business. If you sow potato seed in the ground, you activate at least three laws and at least three things must happen;

1. The ground will obey the law established by Jehovah Elohyim, stating that, when seed is sown into the ground, the ground is to cause it to grow. The ground is not to argue with the seed, nor is it to determine whether it is the right or wrong kind of seed! No Sir! The ground's job description in this covenant is to grow the seed sown. Period! (Genesis 8:22, Galatians 6: 7)

2. The potato seed planted can only produce potatoes! It is *impossible* to harvest beans from a potato seed because seed *must* reproduce after it's own kind! Good seed sown on good ground can only produce a good harvest! Good seed sown on bad ground produces no harvest! Such a waste! On the other hand, bad seed sown on *any* kind of ground produces a bad harvest! Isn't it amazing how weeds can grow

on bad, rock ground while good seed struggles? (Genesis 1:11, 12, Mark 4:3-8, Galatians 6:7)

3. The amount of seed you sow will directly determine the amount of harvest you reap. You cannot sow sparingly and expect to reap bountifully because there is a rule of action that states that if you sow sparingly, you *will* reap sparingly! (2 Corinthians 9:6)

And so we see that God has set some rules of actions, called laws, for us to operate by and get predictable results.

Amazingly enough, He also operates using the same laws! He has 'limited' Himself to His Word!

Notice what the following verse says.

In whom also we have obtained an inheritance, being predestinated according to the purpose of him who worketh all things after the counsel of his own will: Ephesians 1:11

I will worship toward thy holy temple, and praise thy name for thy lovingkindness and for thy truth: for thou hast magnified thy word above all thy name. Psalm 138:2

Surprise, surprise! God works! This may come as a shock to some people who think that God just sits up there on His throne doing nothing! No Sir! God is busy doing stuff! He works and, as His sons, we need to emulate Him by getting some work done!

Notice that God works *all* things after the counsel of His Will. All things means, *all* things. Amen!

The *'counsel of His own will'* is the two Testaments that make up the Bible. What this tells me, is that, if a law is in the Bible, *that* law *is* the standard or the rule of action that God *will* apply and I can know what the result will be! How can I be so sure I know what the result is going to be when God applies a Law from His Word? *Because the application of law brings predictable results!*

Since He has magnified His word above all His Name, we are in good standing while following the rules of action established by His Authority. We can know our outcome when we apply the law of His Word. We shall have what the law says we shall have, harvest what the law says we shall harvest, increase the way the law says we'll increase. Amen. Are you getting anything out of this?

At the beginning of this chapter, I stated that the law of increase presupposes that everyone has something that will to be increased by the application of this law.

Look at the following two Scriptures.

> *Now he that ministereth seed to the sower both minister bread for your food, and multiply your seed sown, and increase the fruits of your righteousness;* 2 Corinthians 9:10

> *Be not deceived; God is not mocked: for whatsoever a man soweth, that shall he also reap.* Galatians 6:7

Everybody has got a seed to sow! God has already said that, it is He who ministers seed to the 'sower', and bread for your food. The main problem with the body of Christ is that most do not differentiate between seed and bread! For the most part, the body of Christ has been eating both the bread as well as the seed! We will look into this a little later, but for now, I want us to fully understand that *everybody* has got a seed to sow!

What about those people who do not have any money to give? Now, who said anything about money? We are talking about *seed,* not money! Seed *must not* necessarily be in the form of money! The reason why you are paid money at the end of the month, or whenever you are paid your salary, is because you have sown your time, effort and skill! Your harvest, then, is a pay-check! If you were to take the same time, effort and skill and sow it in an establishment like the church, your seed has the same significance and productive potential as the person who sowed his seed in cash or check form!

As long as you are alive, I submit to you that you *always* have, and will *always* have, seed to sow! You can sow a smile and receive a harvest of smiles! You can sow kind words and harvest pleasant conversations wherever you go! You can sow some of your clothing and name your seed! You can sow money and expect to harvest money! *Everybody* has got a seed to sow!

The second Scripture I quoted above from the book of Galatians teaches us two valuable lessons. Firstly, we need to understand that *whatsoever* we sow, whether good or bad, is coming up again! If you sow good seed, a good harvest will come to you. The same goes for bad seed! You *cannot* reap 'good' when you have sown 'bad' seed, neither can you reap 'bad' when you have sown 'good' seed. If you have sown 'good', 'bad' *cannot* and *will not* come to you, no matter how bad 'bad' wants to come to you! Even if things don't look as good as you expected, continue doing 'good', for you will reap, in due season, if you faint not! Amen!!

Secondly, *you* reap from what *you* sow! Simple but profound! You won't reap from someone else's sowing, but your own! Take for example the words we speak. Words are seeds that have resultant harvests! In some countries, insults (just words) are enough to get *you* thoroughly beaten up or even killed! Christ said that each one will be judged by every idle word spoken. (Matthew 12:36, 37) By *your* words, shall thou be justified or condemned. In other words, *you* will reap from *your* own seeds and not those of your neighbors'! Watch the kind of seed *you* sow!

God's accounting system: Operating your heavenly account.

Having established that we all have seed to sow, let us now go on and see the double operation of your seed. Whenever you sow, you operate in two realms at the same time!

Watch these Scripture closely.

> *And here men that die receive tithes; but there he receiveth them, of whom it is witnessed that he liveth.* Hebrews 7:8

Lay not up for yourselves treasures upon earth, where moth and rust doth corrupt, and where thieves break through and steal: But lay up for yourselves treasures in heaven, where neither moth nor rust doth corrupt, and where thieves do not break through nor steal: For where your treasure is, there will your heart be also. Matthew 6:19-21

In the quotation from the book of Hebrews, the Bible teaches us that when we pay our tithes *here* on earth to mortal men, (*men that die*) He also receives them *there*, (Heaven) signifying a duo operation of the seed we sow. One seed sown is received in two places at the same time! Wao!

Notice here, also, that Jesus Himself said that we are to lay up for *ourselves* treasures in heaven! That must mean we have accounts in heaven! If not accounts as we know them here on earth, then 'storehouses' with our names on them! This is even more desirable! Accounts? We surely have them in heaven! See what Paul says in the following Scripture.

Now ye Philippians know also, that in the beginning of the gospel, when I departed from Macedonia, no church communicated with me as concerning giving and receiving, but ye only. For even in Thessalonica ye sent once and again unto my necessity. Not because I desire a gift: but I desire fruit that may abound to your account. Philippians 4:15-17

It is important to note that Paul here is talking about the Philippians sowing materials and financial seed into his ministry. Not because he desired a gift but rather, fruit that would be credited to the Philippians' accounts! For their gift to be credited into their accounts, it must presuppose the existence of those accounts! See what he further says to Timothy.

Charge them that are rich in this world, that they be not highminded, nor trust in uncertain riches, but in the living God, who giveth us richly all things to enjoy; That they do good, that they be rich in good works, ready to distribute, willing to communicate; Laying up in store for themselves a good foundation against the time to come, that they may lay hold on eternal life. 1 Timothy 6:17-19

Whatever seeds we sow here on earth, are laid up in store for us in heaven. Even the very hairs on our heads are numbered!

Are not five sparrows sold for two farthings, and not one of them is forgotten before God? But even the very hairs of your head are all numbered. Fear not therefore: ye are of more value than many sparrows. Luke 12:6-7

No matter how receding a hairline you may be having, you hairs are accounted for every time you pass a comb through you hair!

Since we now know that we have accounts in heaven, we need to actively utilize them. Just like you bank account here on earth, we need to realize that we cannot neglect depositing in it lest when we go to withdraw, we are turned away at the counter!

What would you say of a person who opened a bank account four years ago and that was last time the bank teller saw him, either in person or his agent? The only balance he has maintained in the account over the years is the minimum balance permissible to keep the bank from closing the account. And then one day, four years down the road, he strolls up to the bank, and nonchalantly writes a demand note for £1,000,000.00!! I can guarantee you; the bank would not honor his demand note! They would more be inclined to recommend a psychiatrist!

You may be chuckling, but many Christians have been operating their heavenly accounts in a similar fashion!! The last time God saw them was when they opened their accounts upon salvation! After that, they have maintained the minimum balance (their salvation) and that has been about it! And this morning they showed up before God with a £1,000,000.00 demand note! Do you think they are going to get it? Are you kidding me? Unless they steal it, I don't see how else they will get it! However, stealing from heaven is impossible! The last time I looked, they don't let thieves in! We will see more of this latter on in the book.

FORMS OF DEPOSITS

1. Tithing

And it shall be, when thou art come in unto the land which the LORD thy God giveth thee for an inheri-tance, and possessest it, and dwellest therein; That thou shalt take of the first of all the fruit of the earth, which thou shalt bring of thy land that the LORD thy God giveth thee, and shalt put it in a basket, and shalt go unto the place which the LORD thy God shall choose to place his name there. And thou shalt go unto the priest that shall be in those days, and say unto him, I profess this day unto the LORD thy God, that I am come unto the country which the LORD sware unto our fathers for to give us. And the priest shall take the basket out of thine hand, and set it down before the altar of the LORD thy God. And thou shalt speak and say before the LORD thy God, A Syrian ready to perish was my father, and he went down into Egypt, and sojourned there with a few, and became there a nation, great, mighty, and populous: Deuteronomy 26:1-5

There is a constantly repeated command from God to His people found in the Bible. This command is; *'to observe and to do accordingly to all that is written therein'*. In this particular case, He is instructing His people concerning the tithe. From what we read, we understand we are to bring our tithes to the priest (New Testament: five ford ministry offices) and verse five instructs us to *'speak and say'* over and above the act of bringing the material tithe. This *'speaking and saying'* is what is known as *'tithing'* the tithe. The tithe is the material while 'tithing' is the words we speak.

Notice again the command of God. *'And thou shalt speak and say before the LORD thy God'*. Since Jesus Christ is the high Priest of our *confession*, He receives our words *in heaven* and ministers them to the Father on our behalf!

After He is through ministering them to our Father, He turns and gives them to the angels of God to credit our accounts with! This whole operation is the 'tithing' (Words) of the tithe (material). Are you learning something?

Watch the following verse.

When thou hast made an end of tithing all the tithes of thine increase the third year, which is the year of tithing, and hast given it unto the Levite, the stranger, the fatherless, and the widow, that they may eat within thy gates, and be filled; Deuteronomy 26:12

Notice here that, the two words, 'tithing and tithe', are listed side by side. We saw from verse five to eleven of the same chapter that, the speaking we are to do over our material tithe is called 'tithing'. Verse twelve quoted above, talks about ending *'tithing all the tithes'*. This is, as we shall see in the next chapter, because the *'tithe'*, (*which is material substance*), is received by men here on earth. At the same time, *'tithing'* (which *are words spoken over the material substance*), is received by Jesus, the High Priest of our confession, in heaven.

The emphasis at this point is that, tithing or speaking over our material tithe, is the first form of deposit into our heavenly account. So, the next time you get ready to write your tithe check, speak over it, thanking God for saving you and all those good things He does to you.

2.   Tithes and offering

The second form of deposit we need to look at, is in the form of tithes and offerings.

Let us look at Malachi again.

> *Bring ye all the tithes into the storehouse, that there may be meat in mine house, and prove me now herewith, saith the LORD of hosts, if I will not open you the windows of heaven, and pour you out a blessing, that there shall not be room enough to receive it. And I will rebuke the devourer for your sakes, and he shall not destroy the fruits of your ground; neither shall your vine cast her fruit before the time in the field, saith the LORD of hosts.* Malachi 3:10-11

We see here that, when we bring all the tithes in the storehouse, it is so that there may be meat in God's house. And to prove what you put in is what you will withdraw, God says for us to prove, try or test Him! Of course, when He opens those windows of heaven to pour you out a blessing, what you have put in will come back to you with interest! And not the 8% you receive down at your local bank, either! God deals only in folds: thirty fold, sixty fold, hundred fold, even a thousand fold!

I did a research on that phrase, *'windows of heaven'* and I found it listed only three times in the entire Bible! Its first occurrence is Genesis 7:11 when God opened up the windows of heaven and flooded the earth in Noah's day. The second occurrence is Genesis 8:2, when God shut them up to stop the flooding and the third occurrence is Malachi 3:10.

Now, what I see God saying here is that, *when* we bring into the storehouse all our tithes, He *then* opens the windows of heaven and floods us with *a* blessing! Notice it doesn't say, '*blessings*', as in many. It says blessing as in singular! And He says we won't have room enough to handle one! Would you imagine what would happen if He was to pour out two blessings?!

The incredible feature of this truth is that, what many in the body of Christ have been depositing into their heavenly accounts, so far, has been hot air! And when God opens His windows of heaven to pour them out of what they have put in, all they received is a flood of hot air! Scalding hot, too!! Put in some substance, man!

3.   Giving to the ministry

The entire letter of Paul to the Philippians is a partner letter to those who were financially supporting his travelling ministry. In fact, he laments the fact that, no other church communicated with him concerning giving and receiving, except the Philippians' church. (Philippians 4:15) Now, watch what he tells them.

> But I rejoiced in the Lord greatly, that now at the last your care of me hath flourished again; wherein ye were also careful, but ye lacked opportunity.
> Philippians 4:10

Evidently, the Philippians were very willing to sow into Paul's ministry, but lacked opportunity! In this day of modern technology, none in the body of Christ can give excuse of not having opportunity! In a day when one can sow into ministries by cash, check, telegraphic transfers credit cards and even over the phone, there is no way a person can truthfully stand before God and say he lacked opportunity! This too, with the multitude of ministries producing good fruit in the world today, you only need to ask God which ones you need to be sowing into!

The Philippians probably didn't have this problem because there weren't too many 'Pauls' to support, but not any more! Notice what he tells them in the following verses.

Now ye Philippians know also, that in the beginning of the gospel, when I departed from Macedonia, no church communicated with me as concerning giving and receiving, but ye only. For even in Thessalonica ye sent once and again unto my necessity. Not because I desire a gift: but I desire fruit that may abound to your account. Philippians 4:15-17

Notice here that, the Philippians not only sowed into Paul's ministry when he was in town, but also sent aid when he was out of town! This was not because Paul desired a gift, but, rather, fruit that would abound to their account. We should learn not to sow our seeds to those Ministries that whine and cry the loudest, But rather, to the ministries that produce the most! When *you* partner financially with a ministry, that seed goes into *your* account too!

If you are not in financial partnership with a ministry, you have absolutely no foot to stand on before God while quoting Philippians 4:19. You need to read the text in context of what is being said, otherwise you will end up with a pretext (or pretence) Now, you just heard the truth.

4.   Giving to the poor.

The next form of deposit into your heavenly account that we need to look at is giving to the poor.

He that hath pity upon the poor lendeth unto the LORD; and that which he hath given will he pay him again. Proverbs 19:17

When we give to the poor, we lend to the Lord and the Lord will reply with interest! He is not a debtor to any man.

5.   Giving as a 'praise' to God.

We need to come to the point, where, after we have fulfilled all our obligatory giving, we are still looking for an excuse to give! 'Spoiling' to give, so to speak! God has left that door open for us to come and give to Him, just for the fun of it! We can, and should, give to Him as a 'praise' offering, remembering all He has done for us.

Look at the following Psalm

The stone which the builders refused is become the head stone of the corner. This is the LORD'S doing; it is marvellous in our eyes. This is the day which the LORD hath made; we will rejoice and be glad in it. Save now, I beseech thee, O LORD: O LORD, I beseech thee, send now prosperity. Blessed be he that cometh in the name of the LORD: we have blessed you out of the house of the LORD. God is the LORD, which hath shewed us light: bind the sacrifice with cords, even unto the horns of the altar. Thou art my God, and I will praise thee: thou art my God, I will exalt thee. O give thanks unto the LORD; for he is good: for his mercy endureth for ever. Psalm 118:22-29

All of Psalm 118, really, is an excellent psalm of thanks giving. What we see the psalmist doing is binding a sacrifice of thanks giving to the altar, just to give thanks for God's goodness! The Lord has been so good to me, and from the depths of my heart wells up this desire to bring an offering to Him, just to say 'thanks'! Oh, but for the opportunity to come before God just to thank Him! An attitude of gratitude will definitely lift your altitude in God! Go for it!!

Chapter Eight

The
Seasons that
Governs increase

—⚭—

In the natural, every farmer knows that there are seasons that determine whether he has a harvest or not. He knows that he needs to be tilling the ground when the season for tilling the ground comes around. When the season for sowing the seed comes, he better not be caught sleeping! Nor should he be on 'safari' when harvest season comes! The same holds true for operating the spiritual laws of increase.

Notice what the book of the preacher says in the following verse

> *To every thing there is a season, and a time to every purpose under the heaven: A time to be born, and a time to die; a time to plant, and a time to pluck up that which is planted;* Ecclesiastes 3:1, 2

I know that you know what a season is, but for the purpose of our study, let us define it from the Hebrew. It is translated from the word, *'zeman'* (zem-awn'), which means, "an appointed occasions, time". If one is to enter into the harvest season or 'appointed occasion', he must, of necessity, be on time when the season to sow comes! This is because sowing *precedes* harvest! If you miss the sowing season, you can be sure you will have no harvest when harvest season comes around. It is imperative that we keep the appointments so that we may experience increase!

Lets us now examine the spiritual seasons that regulate our harvest.

1.   Season to sow the Word

We need to remember that we are in a kingdom that operates through words! Yes, it is a faith kingdom and faith *must* have a voice and then followed through with corresponding actions! When God desired to harvest light, He *spoke* it into being!

Faith must operate in two places at the same time for it to be effective; in our hearts and in our mouths.

Note what the following Scriptures say.

> *But what saith it? The word is nigh thee, even in thy mouth, and in thy heart: that is, the word of faith, which we preach; That if thou shalt confess with thy mouth the Lord Jesus, and shalt believe in thine heart that God hath raised him from the dead, thou shalt be saved. For with the heart man believeth unto righteousness; and with the mouth confession is made unto salvation.* Romans 10:8-10

> *For verily I say unto you, That whosoever shall say unto this mountain, Be thou removed, and be thou cast into the sea; and shall not doubt in his heart, but shall believe that those things which he saith shall come to pass; he shall have whatsoever he saith.* Mark 11:23

The Word of faith must be alive in our hearts and mouths for kingdom dynamics to ignite! When you desire salvation, you believe in your heart and confess with your mouth, and then you are saved! When you want a mountain moved, you command it to go and be cast into the sea *without* doubting in your heart. The universe is sustained and upheld by the Word of God's power! (Hebrews 1:3)

We live in a word kingdom. We saw earlier on the power of words in *Deuteronomy 26*. We read how we are to 'speak and say' some things over our tithes. When (*and not if*) we bring our tithes and offerings to the five fold ministry gifts, we are to speak and *say* some things over our seed! In the olden days, the Israelites were to speak of their deliverance from Egypt. In our day, we are to speak of our redemption from sin and the wages of sin.

But notice here that speaking was an important part of paying their tithes. In our generation, it is imperative that we speak over our seed!

Let us go to the book of Hebrews again.

> *And here men that die receive tithes; but there he receiveth them, of whom it is witnessed that he liveth.* Hebrews 7:8

We see here that, men that die receive the tithes! In speaking about '*Men that die*' God is talking about the ministers of the five-fold who are mortal men and will one day die. But *there*, He receives them. Where is '*there*' and who is receiving them?

> *Now of the things which we have spoken this is the sum: We have such an high priest, who is set on the right hand of the throne of the Majesty in the heavens; A minister of the sanctuary, and of the true*

tabernacle, which the Lord pitched, and not man. For every high priest is ordained to offer gifts and sacrifices: wherefore it is of necessity that this man have somewhat also to offer. Hebrews 8:1-3

'There', is heaven and Jesus Christ is the High Priest who is receiving our 'tithing'. As our High Priest, He must also have somewhat (*something*) to offer to the Father on our behalf! Since He is in heaven, how is He able to receive our tithes while we are still on earth?

Wherefore, holy brethren, partakers of the heavenly calling, consider the Apostle and High Priest of our profession, Christ Jesus; Hebrews 3:1

Through words! He is the High Priest of our *'profession'*! That word, profession, is the Greek word; *'homologia'*, which means, "acknowledgment or confession." What we say, acknowledge, confess or profess is the very thing Jesus takes to the Father on our behalf!

Let them shout for joy, and be glad, that favour my righteous cause: yea, let them say continually, Let the LORD be magnified, which hath pleasure in the prosperity of his servant. Psalm 35:27

Notice, here that we are to magnify the Lord continuously through *words*, by saying that He takes pleasure in the prosperity of His servants! Words are the number one seeds we sow, so, sow and say on!

2.   Season to meditate the word.

God's formula for success, which He gave Joshua, is still valid day!

This book of the law shall not depart out of thy mouth; but thou shalt meditate therein day and night, that thou mayest observe to do according to all that is written therein: for then thou shalt make thy way prosperous, and then thou shalt have good success. Joshua 1:8

Instead of meditating the problem, meditate the promise! The solution to your problem lies in the promise of God, not in the problem! Instead of rehearshing how dreadful the economy is, how high the inflation is, how scarce money is, how wild the kids are, meditate on the faithfulness of God! God's Word has the antidote of all the negative forces in the world! His Word is the blessing that nullifies the curse. *Think* on His Word!

To experience increase, meditate on the word relating to increase. Even in adverse circumstance, raise the standard of God's Word! Allow your thoughts and meditation to be focused and centred on God's Word, for *then*, you shall make your way prosperous and have good success!

3.   Season to sow the material seed

After you have gone through seasons 1 and 2, don't eat the material seed! Eating your seed is the surest way of guaranteeing you don't receive a harvest!

Then thou shalt say before the LORD thy God, I have brought away the hallowed things out of mine house, and also have given them unto the Levite, ... Deuteronomy 26:13 (a)

But this I say, He which soweth sparingly shall reap also sparingly; and he which soweth bountifully shall reap also bountifully. 2 Corinthians 9:6

Be not deceived; God is not mocked: for whatsoever a man soweth, that shall he also reap. Galatians 6:7

The seed you *sow* determines the harvest you *get*! You sow *no* seed, you can be sure of *no* harvest! When you sow seed, God guarantees a harvest! Sow the seed to the size and measure of your desired harvest!

4.   Water the seed

Having sown the seed, that action should not be the last time we make contact with it! You and I know that, seed in the ground without any water will experience stunted growth and eventually die. We need to stay in touch with our seed through prayer! We water the seed by praying over it in the spirit. Observe what Jesus said in the following verse.

In the last day, that great day of the feast, Jesus stood and cried, saying, If any man thirst, let him come unto me, and drink. He that believeth on me, as the scripture hath said, out of his belly shall flow rivers of living water. John 7:38-39

We need to let the rivers of living water flow from our bellies and onto our seed. Rivers of living water that that will nourish the seed we have sown, bringing it to fruition. This is a decision we have to make.

Paul, in writing to the Corinthians, told them that, it was his choice whether to pray in the spirit or not. Let us look at it.

> *What is it then? I will pray with the spirit, and I will pray with the understanding also: I will sing with the spirit, and I will sing with the understanding also.* 1 Corinthians 14:15

The phrase, *'I will'* indicates that, it is an act of your will whether to pray in the spirit or in the understanding! Make the quality decision to both pray in the spirit as well as in the understanding over your seed.

5.   Growth season

The world we live in today seems to be streaking down fast lane, as fast and as furious as it can possibly go! Today, if you are not on the information super highway, known as the internet, you might be viewed by some as living in the Stone Age! You are probably driving a turbo-charged, multi-valve, multi-cam, V8 engine, 'souped'?? up automobile. Loaded like a jumbo jet, you might say! You more than likely warmed your food in a micro-wave oven in seconds, since you didn't have time to go through the drive-through fast food restaurant! You may be flying your private jet right now, going faster than the speed of sound, watching as CNN brings you breaking news as they happen. To wait until tomorrow so as to read it in the paper, would be *way* too long a wait. And the newspapers have caught on! They have an online edition which you can read online and, more than likely, they will have a special edition by the time you get off that jet!

You see, we are living in a generation that knows very little about patience! Like this story I heard about a guy praying for patience somewhat like this: "Lord, give me patience and give it to me NOW!" The process of time, to many, is wastes of time. They even have phrases like, "I want it like yesterday"!

And this attitude has crept right into the church! We have talented people getting saved today and the minister have them performing on stage 'like yesterday'! We have people getting saved today and preaching 'yesterday'! We have people sowing their seed in the morning and are mad at the preacher, and God, if they haven't received their harvest by the time they get to their cars after the service! We need to understand that there is something known as, *'the process of time!'*

Everything has a due season! Anything coming sooner would be an abortion of the harvest!

Look at what the Bible has to say about this.

> *And he said, So is the kingdom of God, as if a man should cast seed into the ground; And should sleep, and rise night and day, and the seed should spring and grow up, he knoweth not how. For the earth bringeth forth fruit of herself; first the blade, then*

144

the ear, after that the full corn in the ear. But when the fruit is brought forth, immediately he putteth in the sickle, because the harvest is come. Mark 4:26-29

Whenever seed is sown into the ground, it *has to* go through at least three stages as outlined above. I do understand that God does sometimes quicken this process, but I do submit to you that seed *still* goes through the whole process. Look at it.

Behold, the days come, saith the LORD, that the plowman shall overtake the reaper, and the treader of grapes him that soweth seed; and the mountains shall drop sweet wine, and all the hills shall melt. Amos 9:13

What I would like you to see in this verse of Scripture, is that though the speed of the process of growth will have been increased, God does not do away with the process!

Ploughing will still need to be done, seed planted as well as harvested! We will talk more about harvest when we talk about the law of receiving in the next chapter.

SECTION 3

Keys to receiving From God

"Every door comes with a lock.
Get the right keys, man!"
Wangenye

———⌘———

Chapter Nine

The
Law that
Govern receiving

"You are worthy of
Your hire"

Wangenye

———∞∞∞———

Many in the body of Christ have been giving and not receiving as the Word of God promises! And many have gone away offended at God, at the ministry or the preacher who preached it! There could be any number of reasons or combination of reasons as to why they have not received a harvest as they should. My firm belief is that, the main reason is or has been ignorance of what God says concerning receiving. I 'm open to correction, but I would venture to say that very few, if any, receive the fullest extent possible of all the potential harvest of their seed. This chapter is meant to bring you from a zero fold recipient to at least a thirty-fold recipient.

The body of Christ has been accused of having the laziest workers in town! I realize this may not be exactly what some might want to hear, but it sure is the truth! Hello! Hang in there with me. Weeping may endure the night but joy comes in the morning!

Christians are often accused, and, in many cases rightfully so, of being the worst organizations to conduct business with. They are often seen to be the sloppiest, unprofessional, disoriented group of clowns in town! Christian employees are usually the ones that hold the poorest records in their work places. They are often the last people to report to work and the first to leave! The excuse normally is; 'so as to make it for the lunch hour fellowship on time!' If this describes you to a 't', don't be condemned! Repent and learn!

This attitude and habit activates some laws that negate the harvest due to you, even if you had sown good seed!

If you would, please turn to the Word with me and let's learn to receive.

> *And in the same house remain, eating and drinking such things as they give: for the labourer is worthy of his hire. Go not from house to house.* Luke 10:7

Jesus sent out His disciples to labor in His harvest. His instructions were very plain and simple to understand. Labor and as you labor, you are worthy of your hire! If you are a disciple of Christ, you are to participate in His harvest, one way or the other! Regardless of what your occupation may be, you are to contribute to the gathering and salvation of souls, one way or the other! And you are worthy of your hire! How one conducts himself determines what he gets, as well as how he gets it. If he is a lazy, slothful labour, not much will be coming his way, and, when it does come, it may be rotten by the time he harvests it!

This law doesn't just apply to servants in the Lord's vineyard. It applies to everything that you engage yourself in. If you are employed, you are worthy of your hire! An approach of diligence and a pursuit of excellence in all you do will yield bigger harvest. We are now going to study this in the next chapter.

Chapter Ten

A
Pursuit
of Excellence

"You can't put
A man of excellence down!
Wherever he turns, he thrives and Prospers"
Wangenye

———∞———

A pursuit of excellence is one of the main keys to receiving from God!

Look at Daniel!

Forasmuch as an excellent spirit, and knowledge, and understanding, interpreting of dreams, and shewing of hard sentences, and dissolving of doubts, were found in the same Daniel, whom the king named Belteshazzar: now let Daniel be called, and he will shew the interpretation. Daniel 5:12

The first qualification on Daniel's resume' was an excellent spirit! Every other endowment came after that. And because of it, God was able to promote Daniel to one of the highest offices in the land! Are you qualified to receive the pay increase that you have been sowing seed for? Are you qualified for the promotion that you have been asking God for? Are you a person that pursues excellence in all your endeavours? Are you the solution to a problem or are you part of the problem?

Let us continue looking Daniel.

Then this Daniel was preferred above the presidents and princes, because an excellent spirit was in him; and the king thought to set him over the whole realm. Daniel 6:3

Notice here that the main reason why Daniel was preferred above all the other presidents and princes was because an excellent spirit was in him! Can the same be said of you? Are you preferred or are you deferred? How do you serve

God? Do you have an attitude of 'that is good enough' and sweep some dirt under the carpet or are you excellent in ministry?

Remember a man by the name of Joseph in the Bible? His brothers called him 'the dreamer' while his father called him 'my beloved'. Thrown into a pit by his own brothers, sold into slavery but still would not compromise the excellent spirit in him! Whether it was the prison or the palace, Joseph did not forsake his pursuit of excellence! And as a result, God put him in charge wherever he went! God made him the 'head-man' in Potiphar's house. Potiphar's wife had 'designs' on him but he would not compromise his stance of excellence. He maintained his integrity at the cost of his breeches and his liberty! In so doing, he set himself up for Godly promotion!

It matters not if man does not acknowledge or recognize your potential, or even promote you in developing it. Maintain your integrity and the spirit of excellence within you, for God *will* promote you with or without Potiphar's consent!! Dare to be excellent at what is good and innocent of evil. And the God of Peace will soon crush satan underneath your feet! (Romans 16:20)

Joseph was thrown into the dungeons but God put him in charge of the dungeon! You just can't put a man of excellence down! Wherever he turns, he thrives and prospers! God eventually made Joseph the Prime ministry of the entire nation of Egypt! A foreigner lifted up to the highest office in the land! A person of excellence is a prime candidate to receive God's promotion!

Should your current employer not hear and obey God in promoting you, God might just give you your own company!

Chapter Eleven

Diligence!

"The Master key to
Achievement!"

Wangenye

—⚯—

Achievers! Movers! Shakers! These are familiar corporate terms in today's world, describing and referring to those who *make* things happen! If there is a distinguishing characteristic in all those who *make* things happen, it is diligence. In fact diligence is the master key to achievement!

God has a lot to say about diligence and slothfulness.

Look with me in the book of proverbs.

> *I went by the field of the slothful, and by the vineyard of the man void of understanding; And, lo, it was all grown over with thorns, and nettles had covered the face thereof, and the stone wall thereof was broken down. Then I saw, and considered it well: I looked upon it, and received instruction. Yet a little sleep, a little slumber, a little folding of the hands to sleep: So shall thy poverty come as one that travelleth; and thy want as an armed man.* Proverbs 24:30-34

Notice here that, a slothful and lazy man is a man void of understanding! The first thing he doesn't understand is that, though he has planted a vineyard, he will reap no grapes due to his slothfulness! Remember what we said earlier on in the book. The labourer is worth his hire! The slothful man quoted in proverbs will have a bumper harvest of thorns and thistles! Poverty will come on him like a robber.

"But I had sown seed", he might say! Yes, and you are harvesting a bumper crop of poverty, thorns and thistles due to your slothfulness! He should have been working on his farm; weeding and repairing the broken stonewall!

Many in the body of Christ are like the man described above. They are not receiving from their good seeds that they have sown on good ground as they should, due to slothfulness. Some even think they are redeemed from work! No you are not! You are redeemed from the curse, not from work! Since God works, join Him!

Look at another Scripture.

> *The slothful man saith, There is a lion in the way; a lion is in the streets. As the door turneth upon his hinges, so doth the slothful upon his bed. The slothful hideth his hand in his bosom; it grieveth him to bring it again to his mouth. The sluggard is wiser in his own conceit than seven men that can render a reason.* Proverbs 26:13-16

Listen to some of the excuses a slothful can come up with! I ask you, when is the last time you met with a lion *in the streets*? What nerve! All the man wants to do is to get back to bed and turn on it like a door turns on its hinges! The man won't even lift his hand to feed his face! Man!! That is unadulterated, first-class laziness! Have you ever tried persuading a sluggard to do some work? The sluggard will come at you with every argument in the book, justifying why he shouldn't work! He will even pull out a few which aren't in print yet!

The anti-dote of slothfulness is diligence. Notice what happens to the diligent.

He becometh poor that dealeth with a slack hand: but the hand of the diligent maketh rich. He that gathereth in summer is a wise son: but he that sleepeth in harvest is a son that causeth shame. Proverbs 10:4-5

This Scripture answers two questions at the same time. *He becomes poor he who deals with a slack hand but the hand of the diligent makes rich!* 'He becometh poor' means he didn't start out poor! He *became* poor! To me, that talks of a process of *becoming* poor. And it's all down to his attitude towards his work! Dealing with a slack hand is the sure way of becoming poor!

Riches, however, are waiting to be made by those whose hands are diligent. If you are tired of being poor, diligently put your hands to doing something productive, thereby giving God an opportunity to bless it and increase it!

Notice! There is a harvest out there, and the wise ones are out in the fields, bringing it in! In contrast, the slack ones are sleeping!

The soul of the sluggard desireth, and hath nothing: but the soul of the diligent shall be made fat. Proverbs 13:4

The sluggard can desire all he wants, but until he gets up and does something about it, he will have nothing! You can desire to have a worldwide ministry like the one you saw on TV last night, but I can guarantee you one thing, you won't have one just because you desire one! There is a whole lot of labor that went into establishing that ministry.

Notice here, also, that the soul of the diligent is being made fat or anointed!

> *Seest thou a man diligent in his business? he shall stand before kings; he shall not stand before mean men.* Proverbs 22:29

Diligence definitely is the key to achievement and attainment!

Chapter Twelve

Expectation!...

"...The signature
That guarantees reception"
Wangenye

———∞∞∞———

When sowing your seed, what are your expectations? Are you expecting to receive a harvest? Without focusing your expectation, the possibilities of you receiving a harvest are very slim indeed! The reason why this is so, is because expectation is the signature that guarantees' reception.

For surely there is an end; and thine expectation shall not be cut off. Proverbs 23:18

Let us look at the same verse from the amplified version of the Bible.

Surely there is a latter end (a future and a reward), and your hope and expectation shall not cut off. Proverbs 23:18

Notice here that your hope and expectation has a future and a reward! If you are expecting nothing, *'nothing'* will come to you. You will surely have nothing! If you are expecting a good harvest, a good harvest is what you will get. If you are expecting the worst, brace yourself, worst is what you will get!

For the thing which I greatly feared is come upon me, and that which I was afraid of is come unto me. Job 3:25

That which Job *feared* the most, and hence, *expected*, came upon him! Had he not feared his children would be killed, they would not have died before their time! Had he expected his family to turn out well, they would have turned out well! What he *expected* came upon him and what you expect *will* come upon you!

Let us be astute and learn to use the principle in a positive way and to our advantage! Let us greatly expect to receive good harvest from the seed we sow! Expectation is our signature guaranteeing reception!

Someone once said that, an atmosphere of expectancy is the breeding ground of miracles. This is true. The thing foremost in your 'expector', is the most likely thing that will manifest for you! The spiritual world 'locks in' with your expectation, which is closely knit with your faith, and brings the thing expected to manifest in this physical world. The same principle holds true where fear is concerned. You see, faith and fear attract the attention of the realm of the spirit!

So have faith in God, let the spiritual realm respond positively from your positive and expectation. It shall be well with you!

SECTION 4

The purpose for Godly wealth

"Purpose is the anchor
And guide of vision!"

Wangenye

—⊕⊗⊖—

Chapter Thirteen

Getting
The job done

———∞∞∞———

Therefore thou shalt keep the commandments of the LORD thy God, to walk in his ways, and to fear him. For the LORD thy God bringeth thee into a good land, a land of brooks of water, of fountains and depths that spring out of valleys and hills; A land of wheat, and barley, and vines, and fig trees, and pomegranates; a land of oil olive, and honey; A land wherein thou shalt eat bread without scarceness, thou shalt not lack any thing in it; a land whose stones are iron, and out of whose hills thou mayest dig brass. When thou hast eaten and art full, then thou shalt bless the LORD thy God for the good land which he hath given thee. Beware that thou forget not the LORD thy God, in not keeping his commandments, and his judgments, and his statutes, which I command thee this day: Lest when thou hast eaten and art full, and hast built goodly houses, and dwelt therein; And when thy herds and thy flocks multiply, and thy silver and thy gold is multiplied, and all that thou hast is multiplied; Then thine heart be lifted up, and thou forget the LORD thy God, which brought thee forth out of the land of Egypt, from the house of bondage; Who led thee through that great and terrible wilderness, wherein were fiery serpents, and scorpions, and drought, where there was no water; who brought thee forth water out of the rock of flint; Who fed thee in the wilderness with manna, which thy fathers knew not, that he might humble thee, and that he might prove thee, to do thee good at thy latter end; And thou say in thine heart, My power and the might of mine hand hath gotten me this wealth. But thou shalt remember the LORD thy God: for it is he that giveth thee power to get wealth, that he may establish his covenant which he sware unto thy fathers, as it is this day. Deuteronomy 8:6-18

God has absolutely no problem with you eating and living well. In fact, God *expects* you and I to live and eat well!

Notice He says when (*and not if!*) we have eaten bread without scarceness. He wants us to lack for nothing: spirit, soul, body and materially! He wants us to build goodly houses and dwell in them. He has absolutely nothing against you driving a good car! He wants you and I materially prosperous!

He says when (*and not if!*) your herds, flocks, silver and gold are multiplied, we need to keep in mind what the purpose of all that wealth is!

Look with me again at verse 18 of the chapter quoted above.

But thou shalt remember the LORD thy God: for it is he that giveth thee power to get wealth, that he may establish his covenant which he sware unto thy fathers, as it is this day. Deuteronomy 8:18

You shall remember the lord your God, for He is the one who gives you power to get wealth. Yes, wealth! And for what purpose? So that He may establish the covenant, which He swore unto our fathers. Put your thinking cap on and let's go through this slowly.

Notice that God is not establishing a covenant with us but rather, the covenant He swore to our fore fathers. Our covenant with God has been ratified. (brought into effect) by the shed blood of Jesus Christ! (Hebrew 8:6-7, 10:19-23, 1 John 1:7)

Observe what Jesus said in His own very Words!

And he took bread, and gave thanks, and brake it, and gave unto them, saying, This is my body which is given for you: this do in remembrance of me. Likewise also the cup after supper, saying, This cup is the new testament in my blood, which is shed for you. Luke 22:19-20

Weymouth's free rendering makes verse twenty above, abundantly clear. Here is how the Weymouth translation reads.

This cup .... is the new Covenant ratified by my blood which is to be poured out on your behalf.

So, we see that *our* covenant is ratified by the shed blood of Jesus Christ! According to Chambers 20th Century dictionary, one of the definitions of the word, 'established'; is; 'ratified'. If my English serves me right, that would make the word, 'ratified' a synonym of the word, 'established'. This being the case, we can correctly state that, the new covenant is established by the shed blood of Jesus Christ!

What, then, is this *other* covenant God is talking about? Turn with me to Genesis and let us see what Jehovah God told our forefather, Abraham.

> *Now the LORD had said unto Abram, Get thee out of thy country, and from thy kindred, and from thy father's house, unto a land that I will shew thee: And I will make of thee a great nation, and I will bless thee, and make thy name great; and thou shalt be a blessing: And I will bless them that bless thee, and curse him that curseth thee: and in thee shall all families of the earth be blessed.* Genesis 12:1-3

Remember, in Deuteronomy, we saw how God has prospered His people and given them power to get wealth. We saw how they are to eat their bread without scarceness, build goodly houses and so on. But the part we didn't see anything about is the part that God swore to Abraham: "*in thee shall all families of the earth be blessed*". How in the world would God manage to do this and perpetuate this blessing to reach future generations, seeing this is the covenant He swore to Abraham?

Let Scripture confirm Scripture.

> *And the scripture, foreseeing that God would justify the heathen through faith, preached before the gospel unto Abraham, saying, In thee shall all nations be blessed. So then they which be of faith are blessed with faithful Abraham.* Galatians 3:8-9

> *Christ hath redeemed us from the curse of the law, being made a curse for us: for it is written, Cursed is*

every one that hangeth on a tree: That the blessing of Abraham might come on the Gentiles through Jesus Christ; that we might receive the promise of the Spirit through faith. Galatians 3:13-14

We see here that *"in thee shall all families of the earth be blessed"* is talking about reaching all nations with the Word of faith! Watch closely the agency of this blessing! *"That the blessing of Abraham might come on the Gentiles through Jesus Christ;"* It is through Jesus Christ! The agency of blessing is Christ! So, that was *how* God was going to do it!! Bless every nation through Jesus Christ!!!

I submit to you, therefore, that the covenant God is talking about in Deuteronomy 8:18, is reaching all nations with the Gospel of Jesus Christ! The purpose of God in giving us power to get wealth is not only to live in goodly houses, eat well and drive good cars, but to also reach this generation with the Good News of the kingdom! Your wealth is meant to get somebody saved, healed, delivered and taught how to live life to the full in Christ! If you are not using your wealth to propagate the Gospel of the Kingdom, then your wealth is not true wealth nor does it have eternal values!

It is only that which is done *for* Christ and *in* Christ that will last! *Everything* else will pass away.

From whom the whole body fitly joined together and compacted by that which every joint supplieth, according to the effectual working in the measure of every part, maketh increase of the body unto the edifying of itself in love. Ephesians 4:16

Notice that, giving for the purpose of reaching the nations with the Gospel is not the reserve of a few!

Every member of the body of Christ is to be involved in supplying so that the body can increase. We are not going to win the world with the better part of the body of Christ not giving financially as they should!

In fact *not* giving financially for the purpose of spreading the Gospel is a violation of God's covenant of blessings! He has blessed you financially so that you can be a blessing! This is the day for body ministry and everybody needs to be involved! Let us not be out bought or out preached by the muslims or the hindus who are aggressively buying buildings and building mosques!

We, who claim to serve the true and living GOD, Elohiym, Elshaddai, Jehovah, the self-Existent, Eternal One, must rise to the challenge of sacrificially giving for the sake of the Gospel of Christ!

As we conclude, remember that, God's will *still* for you is prosperity!!

PRAYER FOR SALVATION AND THE BAPTISM IN THE HOLY SPIRIT

———∞∞∞———

Heavenly Father, I come to you in Jesus' name. Your Word says that' *...whosoever shall call upon the name of the Lord shall be saved'* (Romans 10:13) I am calling on Your Name now. I ask Jesus to come into my heart and be Lord of my life according to Romans 10:9-10.

> *That if thou shalt confess with thy mouth the Lord Jesus, and shalt believe in thine heart that God hath raised him from the dead, thou shalt be saved. For with the heart man believeth unto righteousness; and with the mouth confession is made unto salvation.*

Now that I'm born again, I qualify for the baptism in the Holy Spirit, with the evidence of speaking in other tongues. Your word says' *....How much more shall your heavenly Father give the Holy Spirit to them that ask him?'* I ask you know to fill me with the Holy Spirit with the evidence of speaking in other tongues according to Acts 2:4

Begin to praise God for saving you and filling you with the Holy Spirit. Boldly speak out those words and syllables that the Holy Spirit gives you. Not in your mother tongue or known language but the one the Holy Spirit you. Remember: YOU are the one doing the speaking as the Holy Spirit gives you the utterance. Continue to praise God every day and your life will never be the same again.

Now that you are a born again, Spirit filled believer, find a good Church that preaches the Word of God and joint yourselves to others of like precious faith. Grow in the Word, for this is the will of God for you in Christ Jesus.

ABOUT THE AUTHOR

―⊶⊷―

D r. Stan Wangenye answered the call of God into full time ministry while pursuing a Ph.D. program in International Economics in 1989. Since then, Stan has extensively been involved in evangelism and church-planting missions in India, Africa and Europe. He joined Jerry Savelle Ministries International, East Africa Division, Nairobi, Kenya, where he served for six years. While at Jerry Savelle Ministries, Stan not only got grounded in the Word of Faith, but also developed a pursuit of excellence in Ministry, which is apparent in his Ministry today.

TV host of 'On Eagles' Wings', an Author, a dynamic, balanced Teacher of the Word, Stan teaches the un-compro-mised Word of God with simplicity, clarity and humor. Born in Nyeri, Kenya, he is now based in the UK where he is the Senior Pastor of *Eagles' Gathering Christian Centre*, a fast growing church reaching London and the UK with 'the Power of His Presence!' A branch of Eagles' Gathering Christian Centre has also been established in Nairobi, Kenya, of which he oversees. He is married to Jemi and they are blessed with two children, Ben and Daisy-June.

LaVergne, TN USA
13 November 2009

164114LV00004B/1/P